CPCU CORE REVIEW 500,

FOUNDATIONS OF RISK MANAGEMENT AND INSURANCE

Dylan H. Kim, CPCU, CFA

First Edition

COPYRIGHT

DISCLAIMER

"CPCU and Chartered Property Casualty Underwriter are trademarks owned by The Institute. The Institute (formerly the American Institute of Chartered Property Casualty Underwriter) does not endorse, promote, review, or warrant the accuracy of the products or services offered by Illi Sharing."

The CPCU Core Review 500 should be used in conjunction with the original readings such as Text, Review Notes, and Course Guide, as set forth by The Institute. The information contained in this Book covers topics contained in the readings referenced by The Institute and is believed to be accurate. However, their accuracy cannot be guaranteed nor is any warranty conveyed as to your ultimate exam success. The authors of the referenced readings have not endorsed or sponsored this book.

The CPCU Core Review 500 may not be copied without written permission from the author. The unauthorized duplication of this book is a violation of global copyright laws and the CPCU Institute Code of Ethics. Your assistance in pursuing potential violators of this law is greatly appreciated.

NOTES FROM THE AUTHOR

Dear CPCU candidates,

Welcome! I am very pleased that you've completed a cost-to-benefit analysis and correctly concluded that this core review is well worth the purchase price.

When all is said and done, you will have invested a couple of months with this subject and paid your hard-earned money to the CPCU Institute to take a one-time examination with either pass or non-pass. Now, that's pressure!

Fear not, this book was written for you. It will help you attain your passing test score and reduce your stress level, as well. This book is unique in that it will not only prepare you to pass the CPCU test, but it will also help you save your time.

In my about 10 years of teaching all the CPCU programs, I've taught hundreds of students who passed CPCU 500 exam with only 50~70 study hours. Today, former candidates continue to contact me to let me know that without my review work, they would not have scored as well as they did on their exams. Now, I've applied all that good experience to the writing of this book.

In contrast to other test materials such as Text book, Review Notes, Course Guide, Quiz Me application, you'll find that all you need to know in order to have passing grade of 70% is summarized and focused in this single review. All the nut-and-bolts concepts and questions you need are inside to fully diagnose your knowledge and polish it up for test day.

Listen, do you want to know the real key to passing the CPCU exam with the minimum study hours? The real key lies in developing your ability to grasp the whole, focus on the main concepts, analysis details in question and answer, and repeat. This review will help you have it all.

However, it should be noted that this book is created as a teaching material for professionals, so it includes all the very intensive contents relating to the actual exam. That means it will be difficult to study alone if you are a beginner who have no experience in Property and Casualty insurance underwriting. If you are a beginner, you need to study Text Book first and can take advantage of this book as a final cleanup. For your information, "CPCU Complete Review" series by the same author will be coming soon for the very beginner to explain all the intensive contents of this book, CPCU Core Review, with easy examples and cartoons.

Thank you and best of luck on the CPCU test!

Dylan H. Kim, CPCU, CFA

CONTENTS

SECTION 7. Insurance Policy Analysis

SECTION 8. Common Policy Concepts

CPCU 500 Exam Guide

SECTION 1. INTRODUCTION TO RISK MANAGEMENT

Topic 1: Quantifying and Classifications of Risk

Topic 2: Financial Consequences of Risk and Risk Management

Topic 3: Loss Exposures and the Benefits of Risk Management

Topic 4: Risk Management Program Goals and Process

Topic 1: Quantifying and Classifications of Risk

CPCU 500 Review Notes / Assignment 1. Introduction to Risk Management / EO 1, 2

1.a. The Two Elements of risk

① Uncertainty of outcomes: Risk involves uncertainty about the type of outcome, the timing of the outcome, or both the type and timing of the outcome. ② Possibility of a negative outcome: At least one of the potential outcomes is negative, which means a loss or reduction in value.

1.b. Possibility and Probability

Possibility indicates that an outcome or event may or may not occur. This doesn't quantify risk; it only verifies that risk exists. Probability, the chance that an outcome or event will occur, quantifies risk. It is measurable and has a value between 0 and 1.

With knowledge of various outcome probabilities, an organization can focus its risk management efforts on risks that could be appropriately managed. The organization can also use probabilities to determine which activities (and associated risks) to do and which risk management techniques to use.

1.c. Classifications of Risk

Classification can deal with assessing risks because many risks within the same classification have similar attributes. Additionally, it can encourage controlling and financing risk, because many risks within the same classification can be controlled or financed with comparable techniques. Classifying risk can also help with the administrative feature of risk management by helping to ensure that risks in the same classifications are less likely to be neglected.

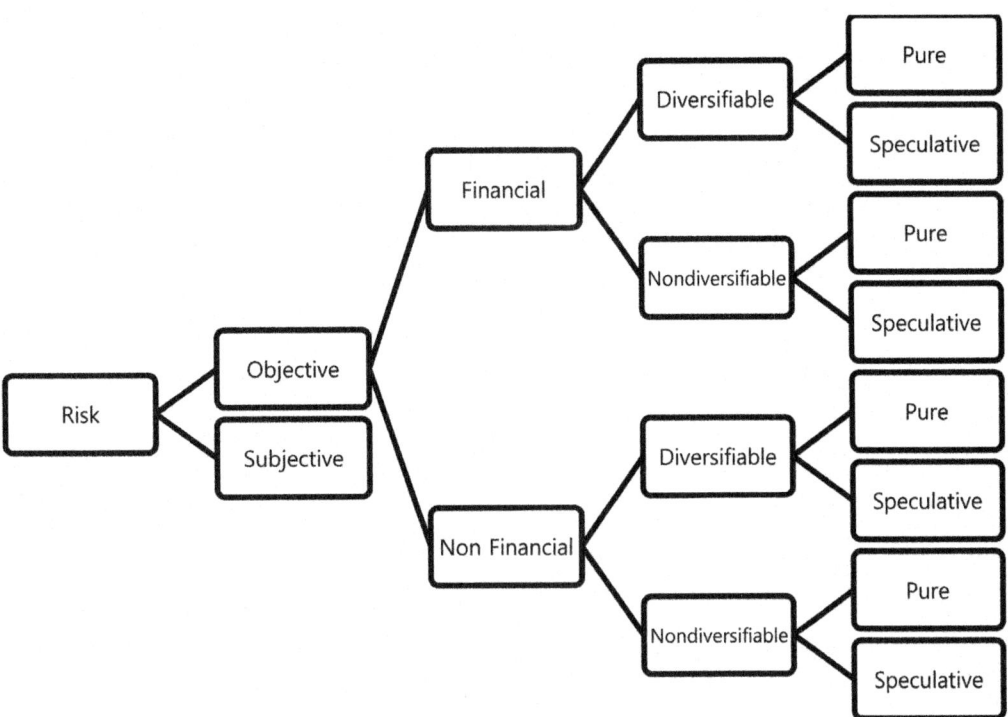

1.d. Subjective and Objective Risk

A subjective risk is considered the perceived quantity of risk based on opinion; as an example, the perceived chance of getting an auto accident.

An objective risk is the measurable variation in uncertain outcomes based upon facts and data for instance, the statistical chance of getting an automobile accident according to past data.

The closer that an individual's or organization's subjective interpretation of risk is to the objective risk, the much more effective their risk management plans will probably be. The assessment of subjective and objective risk may differ for these reasons:

① Familiarity and control: For example, although many people consider air travel (over which they have no control) to carry a high degree of risk, they are much more likely to suffer a serious injury when driving their cars, where the perception of control is much greater.

② Severity over frequency: People generally have two views of low-probability, high-severity events. The first misconception is the "it can't happen to me" view, which is assigning a probability of zero to low-probability events just like natural disasters, murder, fires, accidents, and so on. The second misconception is overstating the probability of a low-probability event, which is common for those who have personally been exposed to the low-probability event previously. This belief may be enhanced by the increased media coverage presented to high-severity events.

1.e. Diversifiable and Nondiversifiable Risk

A diversifiable risk is one that affects only some individuals, businesses, or small groups; for example, the risk of a fire destroying a single factory.

A nondiversifiable risk affects large segments of society at the same time; for example, the risk of inflation increasing the building costs of all factories.

Although private insurance tends to concentrate on diversifiable risks and government insurance is often suitable for nondiversifiable risks, a clear line of demarcation does not exist.

1.f. Pure and Speculative Risk

A pure risk is a possibility of loss or no loss, but no opportunity of gain; such as, a fire in an apartment building.

A speculative risk is a chance of loss, no loss, or gain; for example, buying of stocks. Financial investments, like the buying of shares of stock, contain a unique set of speculative risks. Other business activities may also involve speculative risks, for example price risk and credit risk.

Insurance deals mainly with risks of loss, not risks of gain; that is, with pure risks as opposed to speculative risks. However, many risks include both pure and speculative aspects.

1.g. Quadrants of Risk

① Hazard is a condition that increases the frequency or severity of a loss. Hazard risks are traditionally managed by risk management professionals.

② Operational risks are pure risks that fall outside of the traditional hazard risk category and could jeopardize service-related or manufacturing-related business functions.

③ Financial risks directly affect an organization's financial position via changes in revenue, expenses, business valuation, or the cost or availability of capital

④ Strategic risks are fundamental to an organization's existence and business plan because they have a current or future effect on earnings or capital arising from adverse business decisions, improper implementation of decisions, or lack of responsiveness to changes in the industry or changes in demand.

1.h. Investment Risks

Every investment involves certain speculative risks: ① Inflation risk: the risk associated with the loss of purchasing power because of an overall increase in the economy's price level. ② Market risk: the risk associated with fluctuations in prices of financial securities, such as stocks and bonds. ③ Interest-rate risk: the risk associated with a security's future value due to changes in interest rates. ④ Financial risk: the risk associated with the ownership of securities in a company having a relatively large amount of debt on its balance sheet. If the company defaults on its debt obligations, its creditors might force it into bankruptcy. ⑤ Business risk: the risk associated with the fluctuation in a company's earnings and its ability to pay dividends and interest. ⑥ Liquidity risk: the risk associated with being able to liquidate an investment easily and at a reasonable price.

SECTION 1. Introduction to Commercial Property Insurance

1.1. Quantifying of Risk

Which of the following statements is true with regard to the Quantifying of Risk?

I. The two components of risk are uncertainty of outcomes and chance of a negative outcome.

II. Risk relates to the possibility of a negative outcome. Possibility means the likelihood of an event occurring.

III. The statement "There is a 5 % chance that John will be injured in an car accident while driving to work tomorrow." is an illustration of quantifying loss exposures.

IV. The organization may also use possibility to choose which activities to undertake and which risk management techniques to use.

V. In the context of risk, the chance of being injured while driving to and from work, loading a truck at work, moving furniture at home, or falling in an icy parking lot at the mall are all illustrations of probabilities.

(A) I only

(B) I and II only

(C) III and IV only

(D) V only

Answer

II. Possibility means that an outcome may or may not occur. The possibility that something may occur does not indicate its likelihood of occurring. Probability is the likelihood that an outcome or event will occur.

III. The statement is an example of quantifying risk.

IV. The organization can also use probabilities to decide which activities (and associated risks) to undertake and which risk management techniques to use.

V. All the above are examples of possibilities, because there is no sign of likelihood of occurring.

The correct answer is (A) I only.

1.2. Quantifying of Risk

Which of the following statements is not true with regard to the Quantifying of Risk?

Ronnie Bus Company, Inc. (Ronnie) is a corporation providing shuttle bus transportation to private and public schools in Midland County. Ronnie owns 200 new school buses. Its major rivals are two larger bus firms that operate in the same general area. School districts and private schools generally award annual contracts towards the lowest bidder from among the list of bus companies, additionally they consider overall performance and level of service in their evaluations. Explain how the following elements apply to Ronnie's risks.

I. Ronnie faces uncertainty regarding which contracts it will win (what will occur) or what its risk for next year will be (when it will occur).

II. Ronnie faces the possibility (may or may not happen) of a collision between two loaded school buses.

III. Because Ronnie has a new fleet of buses, the probability (likelihood) of mechanical breakdown is low.

(A) I only

(B) II only

(C) II and III only

(D) None of the above

Answer

The correct answer is (D) None of the above.

1.3. Classifications of Risk

Which of the following statements is not true with regard to the Classifications of Risk?

I.   A pure risk is a chance of loss or no loss, but no chance of gain.

II.   Insurance deals primarily with speculative risk, rather than with pure risk.

III.   Risk can be classified as pure or speculative. Investing in shares of stock is the best example of a speculative risk.

IV.   Subjective risk can exist even where objective risk does not.

V.   Understating the probability of a low-probability event is common for people who have personally been exposed to the low-probability event previously.

(A) I only

(B) II only

(C) II and V only

(D) III and IV only

Answer

II. Insurance deals primarily with risks of loss, not risks of gain; that is, with pure risks rather than speculative risks.

V. People often have two views of low-probability, high-severity events. The first misconception is the "it can't happen to me" view, which is assigning a probability of zero to low-probability events such as natural disasters, murder, fires, accidents, and so on. The second misconception is overstating the probability of a low-probability event, which is common for people who have personally been exposed to the low-probability event previously. This perception may be enhanced by the increased media coverage given to high-severity events.

The correct answer is (C) II and V only.

1.4. Classifications of Risk

Which of the following statements is not true with regard to the Classifications of Risk?

I.   Inflation, unemployment and natural catastrophes, just like hurricanes, are examples of nondiversifiable risk.

II. Diversifiable risks usually do not be correlated thus they can be managed through diversification or spread of risk.

III. Private insurance tends to focus on diversifiable risks; government insurance is often ideal for nondiversifiable risks.

IV. Both the risk of alterations in economic conditions and the risk of changes in commodity prices represent risks that enterprise-wide risk management (ERM) would treat however that traditional risk management would not.

V.   The target of the four enterprise-wide risk management (ERM) risk quadrants differs from the focus of risk classifications in general. Although the classifications of risk deal with some aspect of the risk itself, the four quadrants of risk focus on the determination of whether the risk is diversifiable.

(A) I and II

(B) II and III

(C) IV only

(D) V only

Answer

V. The four quadrants of risk; hazard risks; operational risks; financial risks; strategic risks, focus on source of risk and who has traditionally managed it.

The correct answer is (D) V only.

SECTION 1. Introduction to Commercial Property Insurance

1.5. Classifications of Risk

Which of the following statements is not true with regard to the Classifications of Risk?

I.   Chester has received an inheritance and is deciding how to deal with the money. He has limited his choices to three choices: use the entire inheritance to purchase a yacht; invest the inheritance in a small rental property or home; utilize the entire amount to buy T-bills. In such a case, purchasing a boat is a diversifiable risk; the rental property presents both pure and speculative risk; purchasing T-bills is a speculative risk.

II. Over the past year, International Games Inc. has undertaken four investment capital projects. The company has renovated and renewed one of its aging warehouse buildings. It has purchased the most up-to-date version of its current order processing computer software. It has added two trucks to its fleet of delivery vehicles. Lastly, it has obtained a new production machine that will allow it to start a new product line. In this case, adding the 2 new trucks represents the most speculative risk.

III. Company Lotte is a manufacturer of high profile golf equipment. The risk management professional for Company Lotte is worried about loss of business relating to product design. Failing to answer to changing customer demand and preferences in the design of golf clubs could cost Company Lotte significant share of the market. Categorized based on the enterprise-wide risk management (ERM) quadrants of risk, this exposure to loss would be considered a strategic risk.

(A) I only

(B) II only

(C) III only

(D) None of the above

Answer

II. Purchasing a new production machine represents the most speculative risk, because that will allow the company to launch a product line which can generate additional profits and losses.

The correct answer is (B) II only.

1.6. Classifications of Risk

Which of the following statements is not true with regard to the Classifications of Risk?

I.   The risk of hurricane damage to a business office building is a pure risk for the reason that there is no chance of profit from the damage. The risk is both subjective and objective. The building owner might have his/her own idea about the frequency or severity of loss (subjective), and there are objective measures of frequency as well as severity according to historical data or catastrophe modeling. Hurricane damage to an office building is generally diversifiable since the owner has many insurance options to offset the risk of hurricane damage.

II. The decrease in value to retirement savings is a speculative risk since there is a chance of loss, no loss, or gain on retirement savings. The risk is both subjective and objective. The investor might have his/her own expectations of retirement investments (subjective) together with historical data (objective) on investment returns. The risk is diversifiable since the investor has many investment alternatives to offset the risk of a decrease in retirement savings.

III. The risk of products liability claims against a manufacturer is a pure risk, is both subjective and objective, as well as being diversifiable. The manufacturer can diversify into other products or services to reduce its exposure to products liability claims.

(A) I only

(B) II only

(C) III only

(D) None of the above

Answer

I. Hurricane damage to an office building is usually non-diversifiable because hurricanes affect many properties simultaneously.

The correct answer is (A) I only.

Topic 2: Financial Consequences of Risk and Risk Management

CPCU 500 Review Notes / Assignment 1. Introduction to Risk Management / EO 3, 4

2.a. Financial Consequences of risk

Three components that constitute the financial consequences of risk faced by individuals or organizations are ① expected cost of losses or gains, ② expenditures on risk management, and ③ cost of residual uncertainty.

2.b. Expected Cost of Losses or Gains

Expected costs of loss normally include direct together with indirect costs. The entire effect of losses is significantly greater than the direct losses themselves. Calculating the expected cost of losses or gains for speculative risk is much more complex than computing the cost of pure risk losses due to the wide range of possible outcomes.

The following hidden costs can affect an organization's expected loss costs calculation: ① Time lost by the injured employee ② Time lost by other employees who stop work ③ Time lost by foremen, supervisors, or other executives ④ Time spent on the case by first-aid attendants and hospital department staff (when not paid by the insurer) ⑤ Damage to the machine, tools, or other property or the spoilage of material ⑥ Interference with production, failure to fill orders on time, loss of bonuses, payment of forfeits, and other similar causes of loss ⑦ Continuation of the injured employee's wages after the employee returns to work even though the employee's services may temporarily be worth less than normal value ⑧ Loss of profit on the injured employee's productivity and on the idle machines ⑨ Lost productivity because of employees' excitement or weakened morale resulting from the accident ⑩ Overhead per injured employee that continues while the employee is not productive.

2.c. Expenditures on Risk Management

Expenditures on risk management can include the costs of risk financing techniques, such as purchasing insurance, and of risk control techniques, such as safety measures.

2.d. Cost of Residual Uncertainty

Residual uncertainty is the degree of risk that is still after individuals or organizations implement their risk management programs. The cost of this uncertainty is actually difficult to measure but still may considerably affect the individual or organization. For individuals, the cost of residual uncertainty may include things like lost salary or forgone investment opportunities. For organizations, the cost of residual uncertainty includes the effect that uncertainty has on consumers, investors, and suppliers. For instance, suppliers could be less happy to sell supplies on credit to organizations with considerable amounts of residual uncertainty.

2.e. Purpose and Scope of Risk Management

Risk management relates to the efforts of individuals or organizations to effectively and efficiently assess, control, and finance risk so as to minimize the negative effects of losses or missed opportunities.

Individuals and families often practice risk management informally (purchasing insurance policies and preparing savings plans) without explicitly using a risk management process. In smaller organizations, risk management is not normally a dedicated function, but one of numerous tasks performed by the owner or senior manager. Generally in most large organizations, the risk management function is practiced as an element of a formalized risk management program.

2.f. Traditional Risk Management and Enterprise-Wide Risk Management

Traditional risk management concentrates on loss exposures associated with hazard risk. Traditional risk management for an organization has concentrated on managing safety, purchasing insurance, and also managing financial recovery from losses generated by hazard risk.

Enterprise risk management (ERM) represents a broader view of risk management that includes both hazard risk and business risk, which further encompasses strategic, financial, and operational risks. ERM is a method to managing all of an organization's key risks and opportunities to meet its goals, along with the intent of maximizing the organization's value. An ERM approach allows an organization to integrate all of its risk management activities therefore the risk management process occurs at the enterprise level, as opposed to at the departmental or business unit level.

SECTION 1. Introduction to Risk Management

2.1. Financial Consequences of Risk

Which of the following statements is not true with regard to the Financial Consequences of Risk?

Jenny has purchased a vacation home located in a coastal region of South Florida. The three financial consequences of risk that Jenny is now exposed to with this purchase are:

I.   Expected cost of gain or loss: Based on her new home's exposure to loss from fire, flood, and hurricane damage, Jenny can expect to suffer losses to both the real property and to any personal property in the house.

II.   Expenditures on risk management: Jenny may choose to install hurricane shutters, hurricane roof straps, and other risk control items to reduce the amount of loss that may occur during a hurricane. Jenny will also purchase homeowners insurance on the property.

III. Cost of residual uncertainty: Jenny now has uncertainty regarding the causes, frequency, and severity of loss to her new property. The cost of residual uncertainty can be calculated by subtracting the expected cost of losses or gains from the financial consequences of risk.

(A) I only

(B) II only

(C) III only

(D) None of the above

Answer

III. Residual uncertainty is the level of risk that remains after individuals or organizations implement their risk management plans. Although her risk control efforts can mitigate any losses and she has purchased homeowners insurance, Jenny will still have some uninsured costs associated with any loss.

The correct answer is (C) III only.

2.2. Financial Consequences of Risk

Which of the following statements is not true with regard to the Financial Consequences of Risk?

I. The expected cost of losses is equal to the uninsured portion of any bodily injury or property damage.

II. Residual uncertainty can be minimized, but doing so is costly because more has to be spent on attempts to control or finance the risks involved.

III. Individuals and organizations vary greatly as to how much residual uncertainty they are willing to accept, and this benefits society and the economy.

IV. While designing a display window, Jack, an employee of Meritz Clothing Store, was injured when he fell from a ladder. Jack's accident was witnessed by several customers and employees. Jack suffered a broken leg and was unable to work for several weeks. Time lost by employees who witnessed the accident represents a hidden cost to the clothing store resulting from Jack's accident.

V. Organizations find it difficult to establish a benchmark against which the performance of their risk management program can be assessed because it is difficult to assign a specific value to the cost of residual uncertainty.

(A) I only

(B) II only

(C) III and IV only

(D) V only

Answer

I. Expected costs of loss can include direct as well as indirect costs. The overall effect of losses is much greater than the direct losses themselves.

The correct answer is (A) I only.

Topic 3: Loss Exposures and the Benefits of Risk Management

CPCU 500 Review Notes / Assignment 1. Introduction to Risk Management / EO 5, 6

3.a. Elements of Loss Exposures

Individuals and organizations incur losses when assets they own reduction in value. Situations or conditions that expose assets to loss, no matter whether an actual loss occurs, are called loss exposures.

Elements necessary to describe a loss exposure include the following: ① an asset exposed to loss, ② cause of loss (also called a peril), and ③ financial consequences of that loss.

3.b. Asset exposed to loss

An asset could be anything valuable an individual or organization possesses which is exposed to loss.

Organization's assets; property, investments, money which is owed to the organization, cash, intangible assets, and human resources

Individual's assets; property, investments, money which is owed to the individual, cash, professional qualifications, a unique skill set, and valuable experience

3.c. Cause of loss (peril)

Fire, windstorm, explosion, and theft are examples of causes of loss that present a possibility of loss to property.

Peril is a cause of loss, such as fire, windstorm, explosion, or theft. A hazard is a condition that increases the frequency and/or severity of a loss. Insurers typically define hazards according to four classifications: ① Moral hazard: a condition that increases the frequency and/or severity of loss resulting from a person acting dishonestly, such as exaggerating a loss; ② Morale hazard: a condition that increases the frequency and/or severity of loss resulting from careless or indifferent behavior, such as failing to lock a vehicle; ③ Physical hazard: a condition of property, persons, or operations that increases the frequency and/or severity of loss, such as an icy sidewalk; ④ Legal hazard: a condition of the legal environment that increases the frequency or severity of loss, such as the fact that courts in certain districts are more likely to award large liability settlements.

3.d. Financial consequences of loss

The financial consequences of a loss depend on the type of loss exposure, the cause of the loss, and the loss frequency and severity. Financial consequences vary by degree of certainty and the length of time it takes to discover that a loss has occurred.

SECTION 1. Introduction to Risk Management

3.e. Types of Loss Exposures

For insurance and risk management purposes, loss exposures are typically divided into four types. The elements of loss exposures apply to each of these four types.

Types of loss exposures	Assets exposed to loss	Causes of loss (examples)	Financial consequences of loss
Property loss exposure	• Tangible property • Real property • Personal property • Intangible property Examples: patents, copyrights, and trade secrets	• Lightning or hail • Tornadoes or wind • Water • Theft • Snow or ice • Fire • Mold	The maximum financial consequences limited by the value of the property
Liability loss exposure	Money, including: • Damages or settlement costs • Legal fees • Court costs • Costs of potentially adverse publicity	Claim or suit against the particular organization by another party seeking damages or some other legal remedy	• Theoretically limitless • In practice, consequences limited to the total wealth of the person or organization

Types of loss exposures	Assets exposed to loss	Causes of loss (examples)	Financial consequences of loss
Personnel loss exposure	Value that a key person adds to an organization	• Death • Disability • Retirement • Voluntary separation • Involuntary separation	• Partial or total • Temporary or permanent
Net income loss exposure	Future stream of net income cash flows of the individual or organization	• Property loss • Liability loss • Personnel loss • Losses stemming from business risks	• Reduction in revenues • Increase in expenses • Combination of both

3.f. The Benefits of Risk Management

An organization using an effective risk management program should experience smaller expected losses (less frequent or less severe) and experience less residual uncertainty rather than a comparable organization that does not practice good risk management. As an example, an organization that installs a state-of-the-art security system would expect to get fewer thefts (and as a consequence lower expected losses) and a better sense of security (less residual uncertainty).

3.g. Reducing the Financial Consequences of Risk

The overall financial consequence of risk for a given asset or activity is the sum of the following three costs: ① The cost of the value lost because of actual events that cause a loss; Cost of losses not reimbursed by insurance or other external sources ② The cost of the resources devoted to risk management for that asset or activity; Cost of insurance premiums; Cost of measures to prevent or reduce the size of potential losses; Cost of implementing and administering risk management ③ The cost of residual uncertainty; Cost of external sources of funds, such as interest payments to lenders or transaction costs associated with non insurance indemnity.

3.h. Risk Management Benefits to Individuals, Organizations, and Society

① Benefits to Individuals: Risk management preserves individuals' financial resources by reducing their expected losses. It also reduces the residual uncertainty associated with the risks.

② Benefits to Organizations: Risk management protects an organization's financial resources, making it a much safer and more attractive investment. Confidence that capital is protected against future loss is also appealing to suppliers and customers. By reducing the deterrent effect of risk (minimizing its negative effects), risk management improves an organization's capability to engage in business activities.

③ Benefits to Society: Risk management preserves society's resources. By reducing residual uncertainty, risk management also enhances the allocation of productive resources. Those who own or run an organization tend to be more willing to undertake risky activities since they are better resistant to losses that those activities might have produced. Executives, workers, and suppliers of financial capital tend to be more capable of pursue activities that maximize profits; returns on investments; and, ultimately, wages. Such changes increase productivity within an overall economy and enhance the overall quality of life.

3.1. Elements of Loss Exposures

Which of the following statements is true with regard to Elements of Loss exposures?

I. The financial consequences depend on the type of loss exposure, the cause of loss, and the loss frequency and severity.

II. Despite being frequently reminded otherwise, Samantha was in the habit of leaving her car door unlocked, often with her purse inside. As a result, Samantha's car was stolen, along with her purse. Samantha's behavior is an example of a moral hazard.

III. One of the elements of a loss exposure is an asset exposed to loss. These assets may be tangible or intangible. An example of an intangible asset that an individual may possess is an investment portfolio.

IV. BingBing continues to be unemployed for 6 months, and her unpaid bills are mounting. She recently damaged the front fender of her vehicle right after running off the road. When in search of repairs to the vehicle, she convinced the car body shop to include damages from previous incidents within the estimate. This would permit her to collect extra money from her insurer. From an insurance and risk management perspective, BingBing's behavior is an indication of a morale hazard.

(A) I only

(B) II and III only

(C) III only

(D) IV only

Answer

II. Samantha's behavior is an example of a morale hazard. Moral hazard means a condition that increases the likelihood that a person will intentionally cause or exaggerate a loss. Morale hazard (attitudinal hazard) means a condition of carelessness or indifference that increases the frequency or severity of loss.

III. An investment portfolio is an example of a tangible asset. An example of an intangible asset that an individual may possess is a unique skill set.

IV. BingBing's behavior is indicative of a moral hazard.

The correct answer is (A) I only.

3.2. Types of Loss Exposures

Which of the following statements is not true with regard to Types of Loss Exposures?

I. A loss can result from a property where the person or organization has got a financial interest. The maximum financial consequences restricted by the value of the property.

II. A loss can result from a claim alleging that the person or organization is legally liable for bodily injury and/or property damage. The maximum financial consequences are theoretically limitless, however in practice, consequences limited to the entire wealth of the person or organization.

III. A loss can result from a key person's death, disability, retirement, or resignation that deprives an organization of that person's special skill or knowledge.

IV. Net income loss can result from a decrease in net income, often the result of property, liability, or personnel loss.

(A) I and II only

(B) III only

(C) IV only

(D) None of the above

Answer

The correct answer is (D) none of the above.

3.3. Benefits of Risk Management

Which of the following statements is not true with regard to the Benefits of Risk Management?

I.   Risk management preserves individuals' financial resources by reducing their expected losses. It also reduces the residual uncertainty associated with the risks.

II. Risk management tends to increase the deterrence effect of risk in organizations.

III. Risk management makes those who own or run an organization more willing to undertake risky activities.

IV. The benefits that risk management efforts provide to individuals and organizations are not felt by society in general.

   (A) I and III only

   (B) II and IV only

   (C) III only

   (D) IV only

Answer

II. By reducing the deterrent effect of risk (minimizing its adverse effects), risk management improves an organization's capacity to engage in business activities.

IV. By reducing residual uncertainty, risk management also improves the allocation of productive resources.

The correct answer is (B) II and IV only.

Topic 4: Risk Management Program Goals and Process

CPCU 500 Review Notes / Assignment 1. Introduction to Risk Management / EO 7, 8

4.a. Pre-loss Risk Management Goals

Four pre-loss operational goals supported by an effective and efficient risk management program are as follows:

① Economy of operations: The organization should not incur substantial costs in exchange for slight benefits.

② Tolerable uncertainty: Keeping manage uncertainty about losses at a tolerable level and providing assurances that losses will be within the bounds of what was anticipated.

③ Legality: Satisfying the organization's legal obligations.

④ Social responsibility: Acting ethically and fulfilling obligations to the community and society as a whole.

4.b. Post-loss Risk Management Goals

Possible post-loss goals after a significant foreseeable loss has occurred include the following six:

① Survival: For organizations, survival means resuming operations to some extent after an adverse event. Survival does not necessarily mean returning to the condition that existed before loss.

② Continuity of operations: No loss could be allowed to interrupt the organization's operations for any considerable time. Specific operations whose continuity is vital are assigned maximum tolerable interruption intervals.

③ Profitability: Management may establish a level of profitability that no loss can be allowed to reduce.

④ Earnings stability: Some organizations emphasize maintaining a level of consistent earnings over time.

⑤ Social responsibility: The risk management program should help the organization act ethically and fulfill its obligations to the community and society.

⑥ Growth: An organization seeks to protect its expanding resources so that its path of expansion is not blocked or reversed by loss.

4.c. Conflict Between Goals

Conflicts can arise in implementing pre- and post-loss goals mainly because the goals are interrelated. Post-loss goals contest with pre-loss goals, which makes it difficult for an organization to thoroughly achieve all risk management program goals.

Achieving post-loss goals involves expending risk management resources, which may conflict with the pre-loss goal of economy of operation: ① Tolerable uncertainty might conflict with the goal of economy of operations because the cost of risk management efforts necessary to reduce uncertainty to a tolerable level may be excessive. ② Legality might conflict with the goal of economy of operations because some required safety standards could require substantial expense to implement. ③ Social responsibility might conflict with the goal of economy of operations because obligations such as charitable contributions may be expensive.

4.d. The Six Steps in the Risk Management Process

① Identifying loss exposures ② Analyzing loss exposures ③ Examining feasibility of risk management techniques ④ Selecting the appropriate risk management techniques ⑤ Implementing selected risk management techniques ⑥ Monitoring results and revising the risk management program

4.e. Analyzing Loss Exposures

A risk management professional analyzes loss exposures by estimating the likely significance of the possible losses identified in step one. To develop loss projections and prioritize loss exposures so that resources can be properly allocated, loss exposures are analyzed along the following four dimensions: ① Loss frequency is the number of losses within a specific time period. ② Loss severity is the amount, in dollars, of a loss for a specific occurrence. ③ Total dollar losses is the total dollar amount for all losses for all occurrences during a specific time period. ④ Timing is when losses occur and when loss payments are made.

4.f. Examining the Feasibility of Risk Management Techniques

Risk control and risk financing techniques are considered in combination to cope with the loss exposures. Risk control techniques are utilized to reduce the frequency and severity of loss or make losses more predictable. Risk financing techniques generate funds to finance losses that risk control techniques cannot entirely prevent or reduce.

An organization might use the following forecasts to analyze the costs of a risk management technique: ① A forecast of the dimensions of expected losses ② A forecast, for each feasible combination of risk management techniques, of the effect on the frequency, severity, and timing of these expected losses ③ A forecast of the after-tax costs involved in applying various risk management techniques.

4.g. Selecting the Appropriate Risk Management Techniques

The techniques that best prevent or reduce losses are selected in line with financial and nonfinancial considerations.

Financial considerations lead to the choice of risk management techniques which have the greatest positive (or least negative) impact on the organization's value. The potential costs of leaving a loss exposure completely untreated must be in comparison with the costs of possible risk management techniques.

An organization's value may also originate from ethical and other nonfinancial considerations, for example maintaining operations or peace of mind. Nonfinancial goals can lead to the selection of risk management techniques that, although inconsistent with its value maximization goal, could be ideal for the organization.

4.h. Monitoring Results and Revising the Risk Management Program

Once implemented, a risk management program must be monitored to ensure that it is achieving expected results and revised to accommodate changes in loss exposures. Monitoring and revising the risk management program requires the following four steps:

① Establishing standards of acceptable performance: Adjustments are made for year-to-year variations and events.

② Comparing actual results with these standards: A standard includes target activity levels or results.

③ Correcting substandard performance or revising standards that prove to be unrealistic: Substandard performance should be addressed, and standards may be reexamined and altered.

④ Evaluating standards that have been substantially exceeded: Such standards may not be sufficiently demanding.

SECTION 1. Introduction to Risk Management

4.1. Pre-Loss Risk Management Goals

Which of the following statements is not true with regard to Pre-Loss Risk Management Goals?

I. A successful risk management program should support an organization's pre-loss operational goals. It should help make sure that the organization's legal obligations are satisfied.

II. With regards to providing management with the desired degree of assurance, economy of operations conflict with tolerable uncertainty.

III. The goal of tolerable uncertainty would be to allow managers to make and implement decisions without being unduly affected by uncertainty.

IV. An organization generally should not incur substantial costs in return for slight benefits under its risk management program. By comparing its costs of risk management along with other similar organizations, an organization can measure its pre-loss goal of economy of operations.

V. For public entities such as cities, counties and public utilities, Continuity of operations is normally the most important pre-loss risk management goal.

(A) I and II only

(B) III only

(C) IV only

(D) V only

Answer

V. Continuity of operations is post-loss risk management goal. For public entities such as cities, counties and public utilities, Continuity of operations is normally the most important post-loss risk management goal.

The correct answer is (D) V only.

4.2. Post-Loss Risk Management Goals

Which of the following statements is not true with regard to Post-Loss Risk Management Goals?

I.   Post-loss goals broadly describe the degree of recovery that an organization will strive to reach following a loss.

II. Social responsibility is a post-loss goal that is unique to not-for-profit and public entities.

III. With a post-loss goal of profitability, senior management may establish a minimum amount of profit that no loss can be allowed to reduce.

IV. The goal of earnings stability is that the organization should strive for the highest possible level of profit in the post-loss period.

V.   Economy of operations is most likely to conflict with the post-loss goal of continuity of operations.

(A) I and III only

(B) II and III only

(C) II and IV only

(D) IV and V only

Answer

II. Social responsibility is both a pre-loss and a post-loss risk management goal for many organizations.

IV. The goal of earnings stability is that the organization should strive for maintaining a level of consistent earnings in the post-loss period.

The correct answer is (C) II and IV only.

4.3. Risk Management Process

Which of the following statements is not true with regard to Risk Management Process?

I. Two steps on the risk management process, when combined, constitute the procedure of assessing loss exposures. For that reason, they are maybe the two most essential steps in the process. Both of these steps are identifying loss exposures and analyzing loss exposures.

II. The second step in the risk management process is analyzing loss exposures. Loss exposures are analyzed according to loss frequency, loss severity, total dollar losses, and timing in this step.

III. The risk management techniques selected by for-profit organizations ought to be both effective in meeting the organizations' goals and economical.

IV. After identifying and analyzing loss exposures and evaluating and selecting the appropriate risk management techniques, the next step in the risk management process is to monitor the results.

V. A risk management program must be monitored and periodically revised, and that revision involves four steps. Compare actual results with the established performance standards is one of those four steps.

(A) I only

(B) II and III only

(C) IV only

(D) V only

Answer

IV. the next step in the risk management process is to Implement the selected techniques.

The correct answer is (C) IV only.

4.4. Risk Management Process

Which of the following statements is not true with regard to Risk Management Process?

I.   Monitoring and revising the risk management program requires that activities standards are necessary to obtain a complete picture of the success or failure of a risk management program.

II. Roger owns a computer store. He stores backup media copies of confidential records off site in case there is a fire at the computer store. The risk control technique Roger is using to protect the confidential records is duplication.

III. Yuanyuan and her husband Jack own a saddle shop that has been in Yuanyuan's family for generations. Because of the sentimental value of the shop, they have invested a great deal in loss-prevention devices and safety features to ensure the survival of the business. This tendency to over-invest in loss prevention measures creates the risk that risks that should be transferred are being retained.

(A) I only

(B) II only

(C) III only

(D) None of the above

Answer

III. This tendency to over-invest in loss prevention measures creates the risk that the financial value of the saddle shop is not being maximized.

The correct answer is (C) III only.

SECTION 1. Introduction to Risk Management

SECTION 2. RISK ASSESSMENT

Topic 5: Identifying loss Exposures and Data Requirements

CPCU 500 Review Notes / Assignment 2. Risk Assessment / EO 1, 2

5.a. Structure: Identifying loss Exposures

Document Analysis	1. Risk Assessment Questionnaires and Checklists	Standardized documents published by outside organizations, such as insurers and trade associations, broadly categorize the loss exposures that most organizations typically face.
	2. Financial Statements and Underlying Accounting Records	Financial Statements help identify major categories of loss exposures, such as property, liability, and net income loss exposures.
	3. Contracts	Contracts can help identify an organization's property and liability loss exposures and determine who has assumed responsibility for which loss exposures.
	4. Insurance Policies	Analysis of insurance policies reveals many of an organization's insurable loss exposures. However, this analysis may not show all the loss exposures the organization faces.
	5. Organizational Policies and Records	Loss exposures can be identified using records such as corporate by-laws, board minutes, employee manuals, procedure manuals, mission statements, and risk management policies.
	6. Flowcharts and Organizational Charts	Individual entries on flowcharts can help identify loss exposures such as bottlenecks. Organizational charts can help identify key personnel for whom the organization may have a personnel loss exposure.
	7. Loss Histories	Any past loss can recur unless the organization has had a fundamental change in operations or property owned.

Compliance Review	Compliance review determines an organization's compliance with local, state, and federal statutes and regulations and can therefore help the organization minimize or avoid liability loss exposures associated with noncompliance.
Personal Inspections	Information-gathering visits to critical sites during which particular operations can be discussed with front-line personnel, who are often best placed to identify nonobvious loss exposures.
Expertise Within and Beyond the Organization	Practitioners in fields such as law, finance, statistics, accounting, auditing, and the technology of the organization's industry can be consulted.

5.b. Types of Internal and External Documents

An organization may use the following types of internal and external documents to analyze loss exposures: ① Internal documents: financial statements, accounting records, contracts, insurance policies, policy and procedure manuals, flowcharts and organizational charts, and loss histories ② External documents: questionnaires, checklists, surveys, Web sites, news releases, and reports from external organizations

5.c. Advantage of Questionnaires

The main advantage of questionnaires in assessing loss exposures is that they capture more descriptive information than checklists about amounts or values exposed to loss. Their disadvantage is that they typically require considerable expense, time, and effort to undertake and may still not identify all loss exposures.

5.d. Structure: Data Requirements for Exposure Analysis

Relevant Data	The data for the loss exposures in question must be relevant to the current or future loss exposures.
Complete Data	What constitutes complete data depends largely on the nature of the loss exposure being considered. Having complete information helps the risk management professional isolate the causes of each loss and make reasonably reliable estimates of the dollar amounts of the future losses.
Consistent Data	To reflect past patterns, loss data must be consistent in at least the following two respects: ① It must be collected on a consistent basis for all recorded losses. ② It must be expressed in constant dollars
Organized Data	Data can be organized in a variety of different ways, various listings and arrays of losses can reveal clusters of severe losses or trends.

5.e. Relevant Data

Relevant data which an organization may use to assess the following types of loss exposures: ① Property losses: Data should include the property's repair or replacement cost at the time it is to be restored. ② Liability losses: Data should relate to past claims that are substantially the same as the potential future claims being assessed. ③ Personnel losses: Data must relate to personnel with similar experience and expertise as those being considered as future loss exposures. ④ Net income losses: Data should involve similar reductions in revenue and similar additional expenses to those of the loss exposures under consideration.

5.1. Identifying loss Exposures

Which of the following statements is not true with regard to the Identifying loss Exposures?

I.   The benefit of compliance reviews is the fact they can assist an organization minimize or avoid liability loss exposures.

II. Compliance reviews are a low-cost as well as simple way to identify loss exposures.

III. All of an organization's loss exposures can be identified through personal inspection of critical sites within the organization.

IV. To be effective, personal inspections should be together with discussions with front-line personnel who can identify nonobvious loss exposures.

(A) I and II only

(B) II and III only

(C) III only

(D) IV only

Answer

II. Compliance reviews are expensive and time consuming, and they do not reflect changing regulations.

III. Some loss exposures are best identified by information-gathering visits to critical sites during which particular operations can be discussed with front-line personnel

The correct answer is (B) II and III only.

5.2. Identifying loss Exposures

Which of the following statements is not true with regard to the Identifying loss Exposures?

I.   Liability entries on an organization's balance sheet are particularly helpful to the risk management professional for exploring obligations such as mortgage payments.

II. The completion of standardized questionnaires assists identify loss exposures and shows how those loss exposures support or affect specific organizational goals.

III. The questions contained in questionnaires and checklists designed by insurers relate mainly to loss exposures for which commercial insurance is generally available.

IV. Interviews with employees can elicit information regarding what occurred prior to the inspection, what might be planned in the future, or what could go or has gone wrong.

  (A) I and II only

  (B) II only

  (C) III and IV only

  (D) IV only

Answer

II. Questionnaires capture more descriptive information. However, standardized questionnaires cannot uncover all the loss exposures characteristic of a specific industry or organization.

The correct answer is (B) II only.

5.3. Data Requirements for Exposure Analysis

Which of the following statements is true with regard to the Data Requirements for Exposure Analysis?

I. What comprises complete loss data depends largely on the nature of the loss exposure being considered.

II. Loss data is regarded as being complete when it relates to past claims that are substantially identical to the potential future claims being assessed.

III. Organizing losses by cause of loss is the foundation for developing loss severity distributions or loss trends over time.

IV. Constant dollars reference dollar values today and involve inflating historical values to mirror the consequence of inflation.

V. The data should be collected on a consistent basis for all those recorded losses, and the data must be expressed in constant dollars.

(A) I and IV only

(B) II and V only

(C) III only

(D) I and V only

Answer

II. Loss data is considered to be relevant if it relates to past claims that are substantially the same as the potential future claims being assessed.

III. Organizing losses by size is the foundation for developing loss severity distributions or loss trends over time.

IV. Current dollars refer to dollar values today and involve inflating historical values to reflect the effect of inflation.

The correct answer is (D) I and V only.

5.4. Data Requirements for Exposure Analysis

Which of the following statements is not true with regard to the Data Requirements for Exposure Analysis?

The risk management professional of Hyundai Manufacturing has the following data for losses that have occurred during 2013. The risk management professional for Hyundai Manufacturing were trying to analyze employee injuries for workers compensation purposes.

Date	Loss Amount	Cause
2/6/13	$ 500.00	Customer slip and fall
4/17/13	$ 3,500.00	Damage to sales representative auto
4/17/13	$ 800.00	Sales representative injury in auto accident
6/21/13	$ 7,000.00	Assembly line worker back injury
9/11/13	$ 500.00	Office worker back injury

I.   The relevant data are the 4/17 sales rep injury, the 6/21 assembly line worker injury, and the 9/11 office worker injury.

II. The data are not complete; they do not list the specific cause, time of loss, or treatments used.

III. Because all the data are 2013 data, they are consistent.

IV. Organizing the employee injury data into an array is that; (1) 9/11/09, $500.00; (2) 4/17/09, $800.00; (3) 6/21/09, $7,000.00.

(A) I only

(B) II and III only

(C) IV only

(D) None of the above

Answer

The correct answer is (D) none of the above.

Topic 6: Nature of Probability and Probability Distributions

CPCU 500 Review Notes / Assignment 2. Risk Assessment / EO 3, 4, 5, 6

6.a. Nature of Probability

The probability of an event is the relative frequency with which it can be anticipated to occur in the long run in a stable environment. Any probability can be expressed as being a fraction, percentage, or decimal.

Theoretical probabilities, based upon theoretical principles, are constant so long as the physical conditions that generate them remain unchanged. Empirical probabilities, according to actual experience (historical data), are estimates whose accuracy depends upon the size and representative nature of the samples being studied.

Most probabilities with which insurance professionals deal are empirical probabilities that can change over time as new data are added.

6.b. Law of Large Numbers

Law of large numbers is a mathematical principle expressing that as the number of similar but independent exposure units increases, the relative accuracy of predictions about future outcomes (losses) also increases.

Probability analysis is used to forecast losses when a substantial amount of data on past losses is accessible and fairly stable operations exist so that patterns of past losses presumably will continue in the future.

For accurate forecasts of future events based on the law of large numbers, events must include the following three criteria: ① They must have occurred in the past under substantially identical conditions and have resulted from unchanging, basic causal forces. ② They can be expected to occur in the future under the same, unchanging conditions. ③ They have been, and will continue to be, both independent of one another and sufficiently numerous.

6.c. Probability Distribution

A probability distribution is often a table, chart, or graph that displays estimates of the probability of possible outcomes. Characteristics typical to outcomes of both theoretical and empirical probabilities are that the outcomes are mutually exclusive and collectively exhaustive.

Discrete probability distributions have a finite number of possible outcomes and are typically utilized to analyze how frequently something will occur (frequency). Continuous probability distributions have an unlimited number of possible outcomes and are typically used for severity distributions.

6.d. Using Probability Distribution

The box below shows a hypothetical probability distribution for ILLI Company's theft losses.

Size of losses	Number of losses	Probability	Dollar amount of losses
$0 ~ $1,000	4	4/10 = 0.4	$2,000
$1,001 ~ $2,000	3	3/10 = 0.3	$4,500
$2,001 ~ $3,000	2	2/10 = 0.2	$5,000
$3,000 +	1	1/10 = 0.1	$5,000
Total	10	1.0	$16,500

ILLI's chance of theft loss in anyone of the size of loss ranges is equal to the probability. So, the chances of having theft losses exceeding $3,000 is 10 percent, whereas the chances of having a theft loss of $3,000 or less is relatively large at 90 percent (0.4 + 0.3 + 0.2). Therefore, ILLI's resources might be better spent in reducing the number of smaller frequent losses rather than the number of larger infrequent losses.

Until the number of small losses is contained, increasing the deductible on the company's property policy would not be a sound choice unless premium saved exceeded the dollar losses anticipated.

6.e. Using Central Tendency

After determining empirical probabilities and constructing probability distributions, the insurer or risk management professional can use central tendency to compare and contrast the characteristics of those probability distributions. Many probability distributions cluster around a specific value, which may or might not be in the exact center of the distribution's range of values.

Three common measures of central tendency are as follows: ① Mean is the number of average, often used by a risk management professional as the single best guess to forecast future events. ② Median is the value at the midpoint of a sequential data set with an odd number of values, or the mean of the two middle values. A risk management professional might use the median in selecting retention levels or in selecting upper limits of insurance coverage. ③ Mode is the most frequently occurring value in a distribution. It enables risk management professionals to focus on the outcomes that are the most common.

Similar to the expected value is calculated by weighting each possible outcome by its probability, the mean is calculated by weighting each observed outcome by the relative frequency with which it happens. Mean is the sum of the values in a data set divided by the number of values.

6.f. Using Dispersion

When analyzing probability distributions, insurance and risk management professionals use measures of dispersion to evaluate the credibility of the measures of central tendency utilized in analyzing loss exposures. Dispersion describes the extent to which the distribution is spread out rather than concentrated around the expected value.

Standard deviation (σ) indicates how widely dispersed the values in a distribution are. It provides a measure of how sure an insurance or risk management professional can be in projecting the frequency or severity of losses.

$$\sigma = \sqrt{\frac{\sum_{n=1}^{n=i}(x_i - \mu)^2}{n-1}} \quad \mu = \text{mean, } \sigma = \text{Standard deviation, n = number of outcomes}$$

Coefficient of variation (σ/μ) is used to compare two distributions with different means. It could help an underwriter determine to which account to offer coverage or help a risk management professional determine whether a particular loss control measure has made losses more or less predictable.

SECTION 2. Risk Assessment

6.1. Nature of Probability

Which of the following statements is true with regard to the Nature of Probability?

I. Determining the probability that a certain event will occur is often an important element of exposure analysis in the risk management process. Theoretical probability is the term used for probability that is developed according to actual experience

II. One of the ways in which probabilities can be developed is theoretically. The number of products liability lawsuits that can occur over a particular length of time is an example of an event for which probability can be established theoretically.

III. Probabilities deduced solely from historical data may change as new data are discovered or the environment changes.

IV. The law of large numbers claims that events that have occurred in the past under identical conditions and as a result of unchanging causal forces will increase at a predictable rate into the future.

V. Probability analysis is most effective for organizations that a substantial volume of data on past losses.

(A) I and II only

(B) II and IV only

(C) III and V only

(D) I and V only

Answer

I. Empirical probability is the term used for probability that is developed based on actual experience.

II. The number of products liability lawsuits that can occur over a particular period of time is an example of an event for which probability can be determined actually. The number of times heads can be expected to turn up over multiple coin tosses is an example of an event for which probability can be determined theoretically.

IV. The law of large numbers states that as the number of similar but independent exposure units increases, the relative accuracy of predictions about future outcomes also increases.

The correct answer is (C) III and V only.

6.2. Probability Distributions

Which of the following statements is not true with regard to Probability Distributions?

I.   A probability distribution shows the likelihood of particular future events and an estimate of the financial consequences of each predicted event.

II. Empirical probability distributions provide a mutually exclusive, collectively exhaustive list of outcomes.

III. One way of presenting a continuous probability distribution is to divide the distribution into a countable number of bins (event categories).

IV. Increasing the deductible on the company's property policy would not be a sound choice unless premium saved exceeded the dollar losses anticipated.

(A) I only

(B) II only

(C) III and IV only

(D) None of the above

Answer

I. A probability distribution represents probability estimates for a particular set of circumstances and the probability of each possible outcome.

The correct answer is (A) I only.

6.3. Probability Distributions

The table below represents the probability distribution of auto physical damage losses for a fleet of insured vehicles. Which one of the following statements is not correct with respect to the information it provides?

Size of Loss	Number of Losses	Percentage of Number of Losses
$0 ~ $5,000	8	40%
$5,001 ~ $10,000	7	35%
$10,001 ~ $15,000	2	10%
$15,001 ~ $20,000	2	10%
$20,001 +	1	5%
Total	20	100%

I.   There is a 40% probability of any loss being $5,000 or less.

II. The most frequently occurring value is $0 - $5,000.

III. It represents a continuous probability distribution

IV. The median of loss amount is bigger than the mean of loss amount.

V.   Maintaining a $5,000 deductible would eliminate 40% of total dollar losses.

   (A) I and II only

   (B) II and III only

   (C) III and IV only

   (D) IV and V only

Answer

IV. The median of loss amount is smaller than the mean of loss amount. Because the distribution is skewed to the right and the mean can be bigger by one large loss amount. Mean generally do not resist the skewness, but the median do resist the skewness.

V. Maintaining a $5,000 deductible would eliminate 40% of number of losses not total dollar losses.

The correct answer is (D).

6.4. Using Central Tendency

Which of the following statements is not true with regard to Using Central Tendency?

I. When considering an empirical distribution, the measure of central tendency is called the mean. The mean is the sum of the values in a data set divided by the number of values.

II. The expected value is the term used for the weighted average of all the possible outcomes in a theoretical probability distribution.

III. A probability distribution's median has a cumulative probability of 50 percent.

IV. In an array of historical and adjusted auto physical damage losses, the adjusted amount column is the historical loss amount adjusted to current year dollars using a price index.

V. For a continuous distribution, the mode is the value of the outcome directly beneath the peak of the probability density function.

(A) I and II only

(B) III only

(C) IV only

(D) IV and V only

Answer

III. A symmetrical distribution's median has a cumulative probability of 50 percent, but other probability distribution's median, specially skewed one's, do not have a cumulative probability of 50 percent.

The correct answer is (B) III only.

6.5. Using Central Tendency

Which of the following statements is not true with regard to Using Central Tendency?

I.   When comparing the characteristics of probability distributions, the central tendency is the one single outcome that occurs most frequently.

II. If the distribution is skewed, the mean and median value will be the same as the mode value.

III. Understanding the cumulative probability distribution will enable an insurance or risk management professional to evaluate the effect of various deductibles and policy limits on insured loss exposures.

IV. When a risk management professional knows the mode of a distribution, it allows the professional to focus on the outcomes that are the most common.

V.   Curt is analyzing a probability distribution in which the outcomes are: 2, 2, 4, 6, 6, 6, 7, 7, 7, 7, 8, 8, 8, 9, and 9. The mode for this distribution is 7.

(A) I and II only

(B) III only

(C) IV only

(D) IV and V only

Answer

I. When comparing the characteristics of probability distributions, the measures of central tendency represent the best guess as to what the outcome will be.

II. Only In a symmetrical distribution, the mean and median have the same value.

The correct answer is (A) I and II only.

6.6. Using Dispersion

Which of the following statements is not true with regard to Using Dispersion?

I.   An insurance or risk management professional can make use of dispersion to compare and contrast the characteristics of probability distributions. The larger the dispersion around a distribution's expected value, the higher the likelihood that actual results will fall within a given range of that expected value.

II. When two or more distributions are plotted on a graph, the one with the most sharply peaked curve has the smallest standard deviation.

III. Insurance and risk management professionals use measures of dispersion of the distributions of potential outcomes to get a better understanding of loss exposures being analyzed.

IV. In employing the coefficient of variation when comparing two distributions, if both distributions have the identical mean, then the distribution with the larger standard deviation will have greater variability.

V.   Insurance professionals are able to use measures of dispersion around estimated losses to determine whether to offer insurance coverage to a potential insured.

VI.

   (A) I only

   (B) II and III only

   (C) I and V only

   (D) IV only

Answer

I. The greater the dispersion around a distribution's expected value, the smaller the likelihood that actual results will fall within a given range of that expected value.

The correct answer is (A) I and II only.

6.7. Using Dispersion

Which of the following statements is not true with regard to Using Dispersion?

I.   The coefficient of variation is useful in comparing the variability of distributions that have different shapes, means, or standard deviations.

II. Underwriter Calvin is choosing between account A and account B which both have the same expected loss, but account B has more variation in its possible loss outcomes. Calvin will most likely choose B because there is less risk involved in the loss exposure.

III. The underwriter at Mill Insurance must choose between two accounts to provide insurance coverage. Both accounts have provided a probability distribution based on past losses. Account A's distribution has a mean of $8,500 and a standard deviation of $17,000. Account B's distribution has a mean of $10,000 and a standard deviation of $18,000. The coefficient of variation is used to determine which account has greater variability relative to its mean. Coefficient of variation of A = 17,000/8,500 = 2; coefficient of variation of B = 18,000/10,000 = 1.8. Therefore, A has greater variability.

(A) I only

(B) II only

(C) III only

(D) III and IV only

Answer

II. Calvin will most likely choose A because there is less risk involved in the loss exposure.

The correct answer is (B) II only.

Topic 7: Normal Distribution and Analyzing Loss Exposures

CPCU 500 Review Notes / Assignment 2. Risk Assessment / EO 7, 8

7.a. Normal Distribution

A normal distribution is a probability distribution that, when graphed, generates a bell-shaped curve. It is beneficial to a risk management professional in accurately forecasting the variability around the mean of many physical phenomena.

For any group of possible outcomes that fall within a normal distribution, the percentage of possible outcomes falls within a predictable measure of standard deviations from the mean.

Theoretically, the ordinary distribution assigns some probability greater than zero for every outcome, irrespective of its distance from the mean.

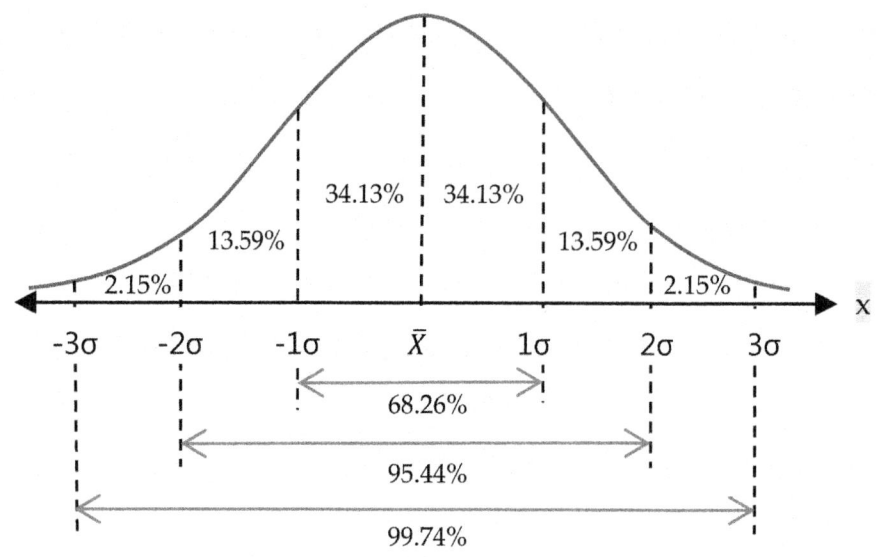

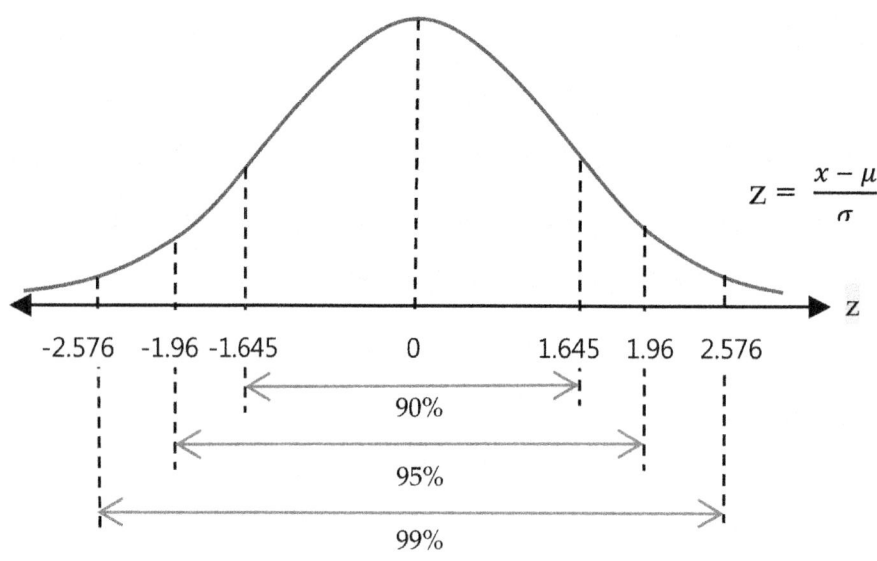

$$Z = \frac{x - \mu}{\sigma}$$

7.b. Practical Application of Normal Distribution

If the normal distribution in the diagram refers to the useful life of chemical fire extinguishers in a manufacturing plant where replacing units too soon is costly, but using old extinguishers becomes ineffective, the characteristics of the normal probability distribution provide a replacement schedule.

Assume that each extinguisher has a useful life of 1,000 days, at which time each extinguisher will have a 50 percent chance of becoming ineffective before it is replaced.

If this is an unacceptable margin of safety, the company must determine what the acceptable margin of safety is and adjust the replacement schedule accordingly.

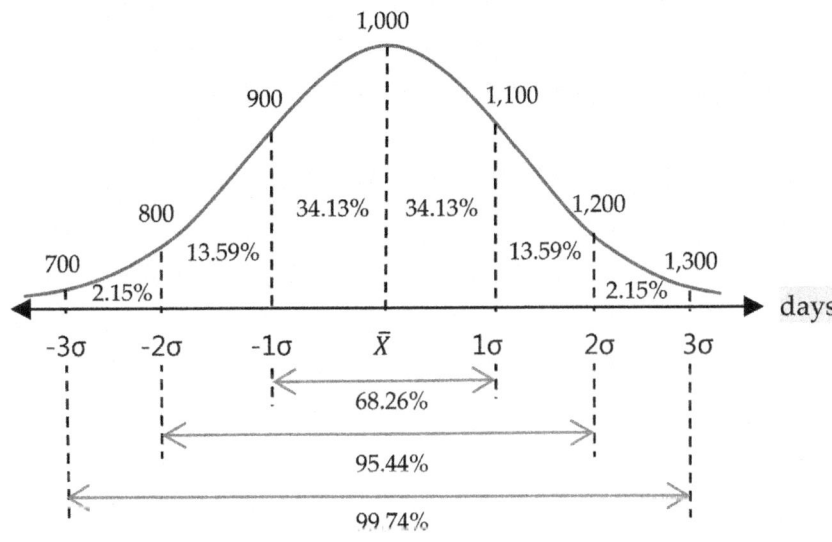

7.c. Structure: Analyzing Loss Exposures

Four Dimensions of a Loss Exposure	Loss Frequency	Number of losses that occur within a specific period. Loss frequency can be projected with a fairly high degree of confidence for some loss exposures in large organizations.
	Loss Severity	Dollar amount of loss for a specific occurrence. MPL can be estimated for property losses to be near the total value of the property. However, some practical assumptions must be made about the MPL in liability cases, such as the maximum amount that would be exposed to loss in similar cases.
	Total Dollar Losses	Total dollar amount of losses for all occurrences during a specific period. Expected total dollar losses can be projected by multiplying expected loss frequency by expected loss severity.
	Timing	When losses occur and when loss payments are made. The timing dimension is significant because money held in reserve to pay for a loss can earn interest until the actual payment is made.
Data Credibility		Evaluation of the credibility of the projections of loss frequency, loss severity, total dollar losses, and timing.

7.d. The Prouty Approach

The Prouty Approach, an approach for categorizing loss frequency and severity, can assist insurance and risk management professionals justify the priority that ought to be placed on certain loss exposures. The Prouty Approach contains four categories of loss frequency and three categories of loss severity.

Loss Frequency		Loss Severity	
1. Almost nil	Extremely unlikely; virtually no possibility	1. Slight	Organization can readily retain each loss exposure.
2. Slight	Could happen but has not happened	2. Significant	Organization cannot retain the loss exposure; therefore, some part of it must be financed.
3. Moderate	Happens occasionally	3. Severe	Organization must finance virtually all of the loss exposure or endanger its survival.
4. Definite	Happens regularly		

7.e. Total Claims Distribution

Another method of jointly considering frequency and severity is to join both frequency and severity distributions into a total claims distribution. A total claims distribution can be used to calculate the measures of central tendency and dispersion and assess the effect that various risk control and risk financing techniques would have on this loss exposure.

7.f. Data Credibility

Data credibility refers to the level of confidence that available data can accurately indicate future losses. Two related issues regarding data credibility may prevent data from being good indicators of future losses: ① The age of the data ② The degree to which data represent actual losses or estimates of losses.

Insurance and risk management professionals can be still having a dilemma answering whether it is wise to use older data, which are accurate but may have been generated in an environment that is substantially distinctive from the that of the period for which they are trying to predict, or to use more recent data and sacrifice some accuracy to maintain the integrity of the environment.

7.1. Normal Distribution

Which of the following statements is not true with regard to Normal Distribution?

I. When graphed, a normal distribution generates a bell-shaped curve.

II. Insurance and risk management professionals use Normal probability distributions to predict future losses, which enable them to marshal the resources to control losses that can be prevented or mitigated and to finance those that can not.

III. In a normal distribution 34.13 percent of all outcomes are within one standard deviation above the mean. If the portion that is between one and two standard deviations above the mean contain 13.59 percent of all outcomes, 47.72% of the total outcomes is in the area between the mean and 2 standard deviations above and below the mean.

IV. If 95.5 percent of all outcomes are within two standard deviations above or below the mean and 2.0 percent of all outcome are between two and three standard deviations above and below the mean, 0.25% of all outcome lie beyond three standard deviations from the mean.

(A) I and II only

(B) II only

(C) III and IV only

(D) IV only

Answer

III. 96% of the total outcomes is in the area between the mean and 2 standard deviations above and below the mean.

IV. 4.3 percent of all outcome are between two and three standard deviations above and below the mean.

The correct answer is (C) III only.

7.2. Normal Distribution

Which of the following statements is not true with regard to Normal Distribution?

I.   In Giselle's large landscaping business, he knows that there is a point where equipment becomes unsafe and difficult to maintain. Giselle realizes that after 2,000 of use, his costs for maintenance on his large mowers and sod busters dramatically rise. Using probability analysis Giselle can better know when to replace equipment.

II. If store owner Zenith accepts a one in ten chance that one of his 20 boilers may explode within a 20 year time period, 18 should be replaced before they become dangerous.

III. An insurer is beginning to write business in a new state. The claim manager, Lee, wants to know how many new claim representatives to hire to accommodate the additional volume of claims. Based on the marketing department's estimate and industry data, Lee has determined the mean number of new claims to be 2,000, with a standard deviation of 1,000 in a normal distribution. If a claim representative can typically adjust 600 claims per year, and Lee wants at least 80 percent certainty that she has enough representatives, 5 representatives she will need to hire.

IV. Assume that Hyundai Manufacturing's total losses per year are normally distributed. The average (mean) of the firm's losses is $500,000, and the standard deviation is $40,000. Assuming underlying conditions do not change, the probability that Hyundai Manufacturing's loss probability would be between $460,000 and $540,000 is 68.26 percent. The probability that Hyundai Manufacturing's loss probability would be between $500,000 and $540,000 is 34.13 percent.

(A) I only

(B) II only

(C) III only

(D) None of the above

Answer

III. 1 standard deviation above the mean indicates 84.13% certainty that she has 5 representatives.

The correct answer is (D) none of the above.

7.3. Analyzing Loss Exposures

Which of the following statements is not true with regard to Analyzing Loss Exposures?

I.   The analysis step of the risk management process involves thinking about the four dimension of a loss exposure. When any of these dimensions of loss exposure analysis involve empirical distributions developed from past losses, the credibility of the data being used needs to be determined.

II. In loss analysis, the Prouty Approach primarily involves loss frequency and severity. The four broad categories of loss frequency and the three loss severity categories are subjective.

III. One way of jointly considering frequency and severity is to join both frequency and severity distributions into a total claims distribution.

IV. One dimension of analyzing loss exposures is timing of losses. The timing of losses is important because funds to pay for losses must be readily available and paid in full for valid claims.

V.   Data credibility relates to the level of confidence that losses that have not occurred in the past will not occur in the future.

(A) I and II only

(B) III only

(C) IV only

(D) IV and V only

Answer

IV. The timing of losses is significant because money held in reserve to pay for a loss can earn interest until the actual payment is made.

V. Data credibility refers to the level of confidence that available data can accurately indicate future losses.

The correct answer is (D) IV and V only.

7.4. Analyzing Loss Exposures

Which of the following statements is not true with regard to Analyzing Loss Exposures?

I.   In theory, liability losses are limited only by the defendant's total wealth.

II.   Two of the most common applications of relative frequency measures in risk management are injuries per person per hour in workers compensation and auto accidents per mile driven.

III. In an array of ten losses, if expected loss frequency is 4.2 when expected loss severity is $200.50, the expected total dollar loss would be $842.10.

IV.   Roger's tire business is operated out of a single warehouse. He has tires, equipment, furniture and supplies at this location. Roger employs 15 individuals at a total cost of $50,000 monthly. The building is valued at $100,000, and the tires and equipment are worth $50,000. The supplies and furniture in the warehouse are worth approximately $5,000. If Roger's property is destroyed and not restored for an entire month, $155,000 is the maximum possible loss.

(A) I only

(B) II and III only

(C) III and IV only

(D) None of the above

Answer

The correct answer is (D) none of the above.

SECTION 2. Risk Assessment

SECTION 3. RISK CONTROL

Topic 8: Risk Control Techniques and Goals

Topic 9: Application of Risk Control Techniques and Business Continuity Management

Topic 8: Risk Control Techniques and Goals

CPCU 500 Review Notes / Assignment 3. Risk Control / EO 1, 2

8.a. Structure: Six Categories of Risk Control Techniques

Technique	Description	Illustration
Avoidance	Cease or never undertake an activity so that the possibility of a loss occurring from that that activity is eliminated side effects.	A pharmaceutical company decides not to produce a drug that has potentially unacceptable effects.
Loss prevention	Reduce the frequency of a particular loss	A company places safety starter-switches on manufacturing equipment that requires two hands to operate in order to prevent injury to fingers or hands.
Loss reduction	Reduce the severity of a particular loss	A company installs fire extinguishers throughout its assembly plant and teaches employees how to use them.
Separation	Isolate loss exposures from one another to minimize the adverse effects of a single loss	A manufacturing company places its engineers and computers in a building located away from manufacturing operations that involve potentially explosive chemicals.
Duplication	Use backups, spares, or copies of critical property, information, or capabilities and keep them in reserve	A company creates a duplicate set of computer records daily and stores those records at an alternate site.
Diversification	Spread loss exposures over numerous projects, products, markets, or regions	A luxury aircraft manufacturer expands its markets by developing planes for industrial and military purposes.

8.b. Avoidance

Proactive avoidance seeks to avoid a loss exposure before it is present, such as by selecting not to get involved in an activity. Reactive avoidance seeks to remove a loss exposure that already exists, for example by discontinuing a current activity. Both avoidance techniques avoid loss exposures from future activities. Reactive avoidance would not eliminate loss exposures from previous activities.

8.c. Loss Reduction

These loss reduction measures control losses in the following ways: ① Pre-loss measures are applied before a loss occurs. They reduce the amount or extent of property damaged and the number of people injured or the extent of injury incurred from a single event. ② Post-loss measures are applied after a loss occurs. They focus on emergency procedures, salvage operations, rehabilitation activities, public relations, or legal defenses to halt the spread or to counter the effects of a loss.

The goal of a disaster recovery plan is to make sure that critical resources are accessible to facilitate an organization's continuity of operations in desperate situations. The plan typically includes backup processes, emergency response, and post-disaster recovery.

8.d. Separation, Duplication, Diversification

The techniques listed would be effective choices for loss reduction in the following situations: ① Separation is appropriate if the organization can operate with only a portion of the separated assets or locations left intact. ② Duplication is appropriate if an entire asset or activity is so important that the consequence of its loss justifies the expense and time of maintaining a duplicate. ③ Diversification is more commonly applied to business risks than to hazard risks. Organizations engage in diversification by providing a variety of products and services that are used by a range of customers.

8.e. Risk Control Goals

Risk control techniques are used to support the following risk control goals: ① Implement Effective and Efficient Risk Control Measures ② Comply With Legal Requirements ③ Promote Life Safety ④ Ensure Business Continuity

8.f. Implement Effective and Efficient Risk Control Measures

A risk control measure is effective if it enables an organization to accomplish desired risk management goals. The effectiveness of risk control measures is often based on both quantitative and qualitative conditions.

A measure is efficient when it is the least expensive of all possible effective measures. The long-term effects should be examined to find out which measures can be implemented with the least total cost to the organization.

An organization's use of cash flow analysis in its selection of risk control measures offers the following advantages: ① Helps achieve the organization's value-maximization goal by providing a basis of comparison for all value-maximizing decisions. ② Increases efficiency by reducing unnecessary expenditures on risk control.

Disadvantages of using cash flow analysis for selection of risk control measures include the following: ① Weakness of the assumptions that often must be made to conduct the analysis ② Difficulty of accurately estimating future cash flows ③ Lack of consideration of nonfinancial goals or selection criteria.

8.g. Comply With Legal Requirements

To comply with legal requirements when choosing risk control measures, an organization should research state or federal statutes regarding fire safety codes, environmental regulations, workers compensation laws, and disability laws. An organization can face fines, sanctions, or liability for failure to comply with legal requirements.

8.h. Promote Life Safety

Life safety is the element of fire safety that concentrates on building standards needed to assure occupants of a safe exit from the burning portion of a building. Development of such standards requires consideration of both the characteristics of the people who occupy buildings and the different types of building occupancies.

When promoting life safety, an organization should consider causes of loss for example fire safety, product safety, building collapse, industrial accidents, environmental pollution, and exposure to hazardous activities that may produce the chance of injury or death.

8.1. Risk Control Techniques

Which of the following statements is not true with regard to the Risk Control Techniques?

I.   A manufacturer that chooses to discontinue a specific product because of potential liability loss exposures is practicing avoidance of the risk control techniques.

II. Automatic sprinklers are a classic illustration of loss prevention of the risk control techniques.

III. Warehousing a company's inventory at different locations in numerous cities is a demonstration of diversification of the risk control techniques.

IV. Within the risk control techniques, diversification is much more commonly placed on managing business risk rather than hazard risk.

V.   Within the risk control techniques, duplication will reduce loss severity and make losses more predictable, without increasing loss frequency.

   (A) I and II only

   (B) II and III only

   (C) III only

   (D) IV only

Answer

II. Automatic sprinklers are a classic example of loss reduction of the risk control techniques.

III. Warehousing a company's inventory at different locations in different cities is an example of separation of the risk control techniques.

The correct answer is (B) II and III only.

8.2. Risk Control Techniques

Which of the following statements is true with regard to the Risk Control Techniques?

I.   Mason manages a tiny ski resort. He notes upon reviewing the injury claims he has received that lots of them occurred on a single slope. To handle this exposure, Mason widens the slope and decreases the steepness. He believes these changes will lower the number of injuries. Mason is employing loss reduction of the risk control techniques.

II. William is a livestock owner who also owns land in a variety of counties. He depends on the proceeds from the sale of his cattle as his primary income source. William makes the decision to disperse his herd over several locations as a way to limit the potential impact from a loss at a single location. The risk control technique William is employing is separation.

III. A manufacturer depends on supplies of a key raw material which it obtains from a particular supplier. The manufacturer makes arrangements with a second supplier to provide the raw material when the primary supplier is unable to do so. The manufacturer is practicing diversification of the risk control techniques.

(A) I only

(B) II only

(C) III only

(D) None of the above

Answer

I. Loss prevention of the risk control techniques is primarily used to reduce the frequency of losses, although it may also mitigate loss severity.

III. The manufacturer is practicing duplication of the risk control techniques.

The correct answer is (B) II only.

8.3. Risk Control Goals

Which of the following statements is not true with regard to Risk Control Goals?

I.   The efficient and effective risk control measures are the cheapest measures that achieve an organization's risk management goals.

II. Besides implementing effective and efficient measures, adhering to legal requirements, and promoting safety, to minimize or eliminate significant business interruptions, whatever their cause, is a purpose of risk control efforts.

III. Given a loss exposure and alternative risk control measures, the risk management professional can select which is most efficient by employing cash flow analysis.

IV. The efficiency of various risk control measures is generally determined based on both quantitative and qualitative standards.

V.   A disadvantage of using cash flow analysis to evaluate the efficiency of alternative risk control measures is that the foundation of comparison varies for each value-maximizing decision.

(A) I and II only

(B) III only

(C) IV only

(D) IV and V only

Answer

IV. The effectiveness of risk control measures is-often based on both quantitative and qualitative standards.

V. An organization's use of cash flow analysis in its selection of risk control measures offers the following advantages: ① Helps achieve the organization's value-maximization goal by providing a basis of comparison for all value-maximizing decisions. ② Increases efficiency by reducing unnecessary expenditures on risk control.

The correct answer is (D) IV and V only.

Topic 9: Application of Risk Control Techniques

CPCU 500 Review Notes / Assignment 3. Risk Control / EO 3, 4

9.a. Property Loss Exposures

The risk control techniques which are most suitable to property loss exposures vary according to the type of property along with the cause of loss threatening the property.

Facing the broad range of property exposed to loss, insurance producers and underwriters commonly examine commercial property loss exposures according to construction, occupancy, protection, and environment (COPE).

9.b. Liability Loss Exposures

These three risk control techniques can be used to control liability losses: ① Avoid the activity that creates the liability loss exposure. However, it is often not practical or not possible to do so. ② Use loss prevention measures to decrease the likelihood of the loss occurring. Limiting the number or magnitude of hazards surrounding the loss exposure can prevent losses. ③ Use loss reduction measures to minimize the effect of a loss that does occur.

9.c. Personnel Loss Exposures

Personnel loss exposures are unavoidable, because all organizations have key employees: ① Loss prevention measures to control work-related injury and illnesses typically involve education, training, and safety measures. ② Loss reduction measures include emergency response training and rehabilitation management. Additional safety training and safety precautions are often cost-effective.

9.d. Net Income Loss Exposures

Net income loss exposures can be associated with property, liability, or personnel loss exposures; therefore, controlling risk relating to such loss exposures indirectly controls net income loss exposures. Net income loss risk control efforts must also focus on long-term effects, such as a loss of market share: ① Separation and duplication risk control measures enable an organization to reduce net income losses by maintaining operations or quickly resuming operations following a loss. ② Diversification is also a viable risk control technique for many because it helps to ensure that an organization's entire income is not dependent on one product or customer.

9.e. Purpose of Business Continuity Management

The aim of business continuity management would be to identify potential threats to an organization and to offer a method for ensuring the organization's continued business operations. Business continuity management is made to fulfill the organizational post-loss goals of survival and continuity of operations.

9.f. Scope of Business Continuity Management

Business continuity management can address the subsequent potential situations in order to help achieve an organization's goal of survival and continuity of operations following a loss: interruptions from property losses, information technology (IT) problems, human failures (such as fraud), loss of utility services or infrastructure, reputation losses, and human asset (personnel) losses.

9.g. Business Continuity Process

The following are the six steps in the business continuity process: ① Identify the organization's critical functions ② Identify the risks (threats) to the organization's critical functions ③ Evaluate the effect of the risks on those critical functions ④ Develop a business continuity strategy ⑤ Develop a business continuity plan ⑥ Monitor and revise the business continuity process.

9.h. Guidelines for Design of Business Continuity Plan

Guidelines for design of an effective business continuity plan include the following: ① Design a clear plan that can be quickly read and understood ② Provide copies of the plan to all relevant parties ③ Provide appropriate training, including periodic rehearsals of crisis procedures

9.i. Common Contents of Business Continuity Plan

Business continuity plans commonly contain the following content: ① Strategy the organization will follow to manage the crisis ② Information about the roles and duties of various individuals in the organization ③ Steps that can be taken to prevent any further loss or damage ④ Emergency response plan to deal with life and safety issues ⑤ Crisis management plan to deal with communication and reputation issues ⑥ Business recovery and restoration plan to deal with losses to property, processes, or products ⑦ Access to stress management and counseling for affected parties

9.1. Application of Risk Control Techniques

Which of the following statements is not true with the application of Risk Control Techniques?

I.   Limiting the number of key employees who are able to travel on a single aircraft is an illustration of separation of the risk control techniques.

II.   Measures that control property, liability, or personnel loss exposures are ineffective in managing net income loss exposures.

III. Two risk control measures which are directly targeted at reducing the severity of net income losses are separation and duplication.

IV.   Three risk control techniques can be employed effectively to control liability losses. Avoidance, loss prevention, and diversification are those three techniques.

V.   Commercial property loss exposures are generally examined according to construction, occupancy, protection, and environment.

(A) I and III only

(B) II and IV only

(C) III and V only

(D) I and V only

Answer

II. Net income loss exposures can be associated with property, liability, or personnel loss exposures. Therefore, controlling risk relating to such loss exposures indirectly controls net income loss exposures.

IV. Three risk control techniques can be used effectively to control liability losses. Avoidance, loss prevention, and loss reduction are those three techniques.

The correct answer is (B) II and IV only.

9.2. Application of Risk Control Techniques

Which of the following statements is not true with the Application of Risk Control Techniques?

The Sergeant Pharmaceutical Company manufactures and distributes both prescription medications and medicines sold non-prescription by pharmacies and other outlets. Over fifty percent of Sergeant's annual expenses are for development and research of brand new products. About 50 % of Sergeant's revenues come from an ulcer remedy. Management is worried that any prolonged absence of their ulcer medicine from the market would cause doctors to prescribe another brand, and they might not go back to Sergeant's brand when it becomes available again. The testing process for some products is oftentimes involving a number of years of testing on dogs, primates, or other relatively long-lived animals. Sergeant stores its research records in fire-resistive filing cabinets in the records room of its research center. The center also houses research laboratories, offices for research personnel, and animals for research. The research center is situated in a sprinklered, fire-resistive building alongside Sergeant's factory. Personnel who handle the animals are thoroughly trained in animal care to guarantee the safety of both the animals and employees.

I.   The risk control measures Sergeant is currently using for property loss exposures-using fire-resistive construction and sprinklers.

II. The risk control measures Sergeant is currently using for personnel loss exposures-thorough training of staff handling animals.

III. The risk control measures Sergeant is currently using for net income loss exposures-in addition to the risk control measures just mentioned, Sergeant's diversification of product offerings through research and development of new products reduces the net income exposure related to the ulcer remedy.

(A) I only

(B) II only

(C) III only

(D) None of the above

Answer

The correct answer is (D) none of the above.

9.3. Business Continuity Management

Which of the following statements is true with the Business Continuity Management?

I.   Arrange appropriate insurance policy is one of the steps in the business continuity process.

II. Business continuity management is primarily created to meet survival of the risk management goals.

III. Business continuity management was created to be used during a crisis, so it should be clear and able to be quickly read and understood.

IV. Dylan has developed a business continuity plan to address the threat of the loss of utility services at his company's large manufacturing facility. The management team has reviewed his plan and agrees that the plan can be quickly read and understood and should be effective in the event of a crisis. Dylan has provided copies of the plan to all relevant parties. Dylan's next step should be developing a business recovery and restoration plan.

(A) I and II only

(B) II and III only

(C) III and IV only

(D) I and IV only

Answer

I. Arrange appropriate insurance coverage is not included the steps in the business continuity process

IV. Dylan's next step should be providing training and periodic rehearsals of the procedures.

The correct answer is (B) II and III only.

SECTION 3. Risk Control

SECTION 4. RISK FINANCING

Topic 10: Risk Financing Goals and Measures

Topic 11: Risk Financing Measures

Topic 10: Risk Financing Goals and Measures

CPCU 500 Review Notes / Assignment 4. Risk Financing / EO 1, 2, 3

10.a. Structure: Risk Financing Goals

Because risk financing is an integral part of a risk management program, risk financing goals should support risk management program goals. Common risk financing goals include these five.

1. Pay for Losses	Funds should be available to pay for losses when they occur so as not to disrupt normal activities. Paying for losses includes paying transfer costs (such as insurance premiums) when losses are transferred to another party.
2. Manage the Cost of Risk	① Administrative expenses: include the cost of internal administration and the cost of purchased services, such as claim administration and risk management consulting. ② Risk control expenses: incurred to reduce loss frequency, reduce the severity of losses, or increase the predictability of future losses. ③ Risk financing expenses: incurred to manage the risk financing measures used to meet risk financing goals. Many of these risk financing measures involve transaction costs, including commissions paid to brokers, fees paid to banks or other investment institutions in order to establish accounts, and fees paid for trades on capital market transactions.

3. Manage Cash Flow Variability	An organization's maximum cash flow variability level depends on the organization's size, its financial strength, management's degree of risk tolerance, and the degree to which the organization's stakeholders are willing to accept risk.
4. Maintain an Appropriate Level of Liquidity	A certain level of cash liquidity (liquid assets) is required to pay for retained losses. A liquid asset is one that can easily be converted into cash.
5. Comply With Legal Requirements	Some laws and regulations require specific risk financing measures. Legal requirements can also affect how risk financing measures are implemented. In addition, contractual obligations, such as leases on automobiles or aircraft, may also require insurance coverage on the leased property.

10.b. Aspects of Retention and Transfer

Since the majority of risk financing measures involve factors of both retention and transfer, the distinction between the two is eroding. Pure retention and pure transfer can be regarded as the extreme points on a continuum of risk financing measures, with virtually all risk financing measures, including insurance, falling somewhere between the two extremes.

10.c. Planned and Unplanned Retention

Planned retention is surely an intentional form of financing risks which have been adequately identified and analyzed. Planned retention permits the risk management professional to select the most suitable retention funding measure.

Unplanned retention occurs either when losses cannot be insured or in any manner transferred or when an individual or organization neglects to identify or assess a loss exposure. Unplanned retention may have a severe impact on risk financing goals and limits the option of retention funding techniques.

10.d. Planned Retention Funding Techniques

The four planned retention funding techniques available to an organization are as follows: ① Current expensing of losses: an approach that relies on current cash flows to cover the cost of losses ② Using an unfunded reserve: an accounting entry recognizing the organization's potential liability to pay for a loss, but not specifying the assets that are to pay for a potential loss ③ Using a funded reserve: a reserve supported with cash, securities, or other liquid assets allocated to meet the obligations that the reserve represents ④ Borrowing funds: an approach that indirectly uses an organization's own resources to pay for losses and in time uses its own earnings to repay the loan.

10.e. Advantages of Retention

The advantages of using retention as a risk financing technique include ① Cost savings: retention is typically the most economical risk financing alternative because many costs involved in transfer are avoided. ② Control of the claims process: this control allows greater flexibility in investigating and negotiating claim settlements. ③ Timing of cash flows: retention avoids the up-front payment of most transfer measures (such as insurance) and can shorten the delay between the time of loss and the payment by the other party. ④ Incentives for risk control: When individuals or organizations directly pay for their own losses, they have a strong incentive to prevent and reduce those losses.

10.f. Transfer

A pure transfer shifts the responsibility for the entire loss from one party (transferor) to another party (transferee). Most, if not all, transfer arrangements contain limitations that prevent them from being regarded as pure transfers: ① Risk transfer measures typically include some combination of retention and transfer. The potential loss amounts that are transferred are limited by deductibles, limits, or other restrictions, so that the transferor pays at least some portion of the loss. ② The ultimate responsibility for paying for the loss remains with the individual or organization. If the other party (such as an insurer) cannot or will not pay for a loss, the loss must be absorbed by the individual or organization.

10.g. Advantages of Transfer

There are significant advantages to using risk transfer measures as part of a risk financing program, including these: ① Reducing exposure to large losses ② Reducing cash flow variability: reduced variability of cash flows and earnings on those cash flows increases the overall value of the organization ③ Providing ancillary services: for example, insurers often offer risk assessment and control services as well as claim administration and litigation services. ④ Avoiding adverse employee and public relations: issues with claim administration are less likely to harm the reputation of the organization.

10.h. Mix of Retention and Transfer

An organization's risk financing program would need to balance retention and transfer considering the particular risk financing goals that the organization is trying to achieve. This balance can be accomplished through the appropriate combination of risk financing measures.

Using retention to satisfy risk financing goals could possibly be the most cost effective risk financing measure, depending on how the organization structures and manages its retention. Using transfer to fulfill risk financing goals typically provides the organization the greatest certainty regarding its capacity to pay losses and the greatest cash flow certainty and is also beneficial in preventing liquidity problems.

10.i. Loss Exposure Characteristics

Frequency and severity are two loss exposure characteristics that assist an organization select which loss exposures to retain and which to transfer. For most loss exposures, risk financing through retention is suitable. For low-frequency, high-severity loss exposures, risk transfer measures are suitable.

	Low Frequency	High Frequency
Low Severity	Retain	Retain
High Severity	Transfer	Avoid (if possible) Retain (last resort)

10.j. Organization Specific Characteristics

The ideal balance between retention and transfer varies for each individual or organization, according to specific characteristics. The individual or organization specific characteristics that can impact the selection of appropriate risk financing measures include things like the below.

1. Risk tolerance	Generally, the higher an individual's or organization's willingness to accept risk, the higher the likelihood that more risk will be retained.
2. Financial condition	The more financially secure an individual or organization is, the more loss exposures it can retain without causing liquidity or cash flow variability problems.
3. Core operations	An organization is better able to retain loss exposures directly related to its core operations.
4. Ability to diversify	If an organization can diversify its loss exposures, it can offset losses that occur and can more accurately forecast future losses.
5. Ability to control losses	The more risk control an organization can undertake, the more loss exposures it can typically retain.
6. Ability to administer the retention plan	Organizations that can fulfill the greater administrative requirements of retention (claim administration, risk management consulting, or retention fund accounting) can use retention more efficiently.

10.1. Risk Financing Goals

Which of the following statements is not true with regard to the Risk Financing Goals?

I.   The level of cash flow variability that an organization would prefer to accept is impacted by the risk appetite of its stakeholders.

II. As being an organization's retention level increases, so does the degree of liquidity required.

III. The suitable cash flow variability level for an organization depends upon factors including its size and financial strength.

IV. For the majority of organizations, borrowing is the only accessible way of increasing liquidity to pay for retained losses.

V.   Administrative expenses include commissions paid to brokers, fees paid to banks or other investment institutions as a way to establish accounts, and fees paid for trades on capital market transactions.

(A) I and II only

(B) II and III only

(C) III and IV only

(D) IV and V only

Answer

IV. An organization might use the following methods to increase cash liquidity: ① Internal method: selling assets or retaining cash flow ② External method: borrowing, issuing a debt instrument, or issuing stock

V. Risk financing expenses involve transaction costs, including commissions paid to brokers, fees paid to banks or other investment institutions in order to establish accounts, and fees paid for trades on capital market transactions.

The correct answer is (D) IV and V only.

10.2. Retention and Transfer

Which of the following statements is true with regard to the Risk Financing Goals?

I.   A funded reserve is a planned retention funding measure that recognizes in advance the chance of loss, and supports that potential by allocating cash, securities, or other liquid assets to fulfill obligations.

II. Timing of cash flows is recognized as an advantage of using retention as a risk financing technique.

III. Using an unfunded reserve is the least formal and the most economical to administer.

IV. Risk transfers shift the transferor's legal responsibility for paying a loss to the transferee.

V.   Risk transfer measures have a tendency to increase the variability of cash flow making an organization less attractive to investors.

  (A) I and II only

  (B) I and III only

  (C) II and IV only

  (D) II and V only

Answer

III. Current expensing of losses is the least formal and the least expensive planned retention funding measure to administer.

IV. The ultimate responsibility for paying for loss remains with the transferor in a risk transfer agreement.

V. There are significant advantages to using risk transfer measures as part of a risk financing program, including reducing cash flow variability. Reduced variability of cash flows and earnings on those cash flows makes publicly traded organizations more attractive to investors and potentially increases the overall value of the organization.

The correct answer is (A) I and II only.

10.3. Risk Financing Measures

Which of the following statements is not true with regard to the Risk Financing Measures?

I. It is normally less costly for an organization to retain rather than transfer loss exposures directly related to its primary operations.

II. Risk transfer measures are most suitable for losses that exhibit low-frequency, high-severity patterns.

III. Retention enables an organization to control its cost of risk and also, is the most effective way to meet the risk financing goal of paying losses.

IV. The ideal balance between retention and transfer varies for each organization, according to specific characteristics. Everything else being equal, the more risk control an organization undertakes, the much more likely its ability to fund the retention of the affected exposures.

(A) I and II only

(B) III only

(C) IV only

(D) None of the above

Answer

III. The primary benefit of transfer is certainty regarding the ability to pay losses.

The correct answer is (B) III only.

Topic 11: Risk Financing Measures

CPCU 500 Review Notes / Assignment 4. Risk Financing / EO 4

11.a. Structure: Summary of Risk Financing Measures

	1. Pay for Losses	2. Manage the Cost of Risk	3. Manage Cash Flow Variability	4. Maintain an Appropriate Level of Liquidity	5. Comply With Legal Requirements
Retrospective Rating Plans	O	O	O	△	O
Large Deductible Plans	O	O	△	△	O
Guaranteed Cost Insurance	△	△	O	O	O
Pools	O	O	O	△	△
Hold-Harmless Agreement	△	△	△	O	△
Captive Insurers	△	△	O	△	△
Finite Risk Plan	O	O	O	X	O
Capital Market Solutions	△	X	O	O	△
Self-Insurance	△	△	X	△	O

11.b. Retrospective Rating Plans

A risk financing plan to which a business buys insurance controlled by a rating plan that adjusts the premium rate after the end of the policy period based on a portion of the insured's actual losses during the policy period.

Such plans are employed to finance low-to-medium severity losses and are generally mixed with other risk financing plans to cover high-severity losses. An organization should have a substantial insurance premium to benefit from a retrospective rating plan.

1. Pay for Losses	O	Because the insurer pays for losses as they become due
2. Manage the Cost of Risk	O	Because it includes a significant amount of retention and can reduce an organization's cost of risk over the long run
3. Manage Cash Flow Variability	O	Because it helps manage some cash flow uncertainty
4. Maintain an Appropriate Level of Liquidity	△	If the loss limit and maximum premium are chosen carefully
5. Comply With Legal Requirements	O	Because an insurer issues a policy guaranteeing that all covered claims will be paid

11.c. Large Deductible Plans

An insurance policy having a per occurrence or per accident deductible of $100,000 or higher.

The insurer adjusts and pays all claims, even those under the deductible level, and then seeks repayment from the insured for those claims that fall under the deductible.

1. Pay for Losses	O	Because the insurer pays for losses as they become due, including losses for which the insured eventually reimburses the insurer.
2. Manage the Cost of Risk	O	Because the insurer administers the claim process, even for the small claims the insurer has retained.
3. Manage Cash Flow Variability	△	If the deductible amount is chosen carefully.
4. Maintain an Appropriate Level of Liquidity	△	If the deductible amount is chosen carefully.
5. Comply With Legal Requirements	O	Because an insurer issues a policy guaranteeing that all covered claims will be paid.

11.d. Guaranteed Cost Insurance

An insurance policy in which the premium and limits are specified in advance.

The insurance buyer (insured) transfers the potential financial consequences of certain loss exposures to an insurer and pays the insurer a comparatively small, certain financial cost in the form of an insurance premium. In return, the insurer agrees to pay for all the organization's losses which are covered by the insurance policy, generally subject to a deductible and policy limit. The insurer also agrees to provide necessary services, for example claim handling and liability-claim defense.

1. Pay for Losses	△	If the loss exposures are covered
2. Manage the Cost of Risk	△	To some degree because insurance premiums include insurers' expenses
3. Manage Cash Flow Variability	O	Because uncertainty about future losses is transferred to the insurer
4. Maintain an Appropriate Level of Liquidity	O	Because the organization requires less liquidity than with retention or other risk financing
5. Comply With Legal Requirements	O	Yes

11.e. Pools

A group of organizations that insure each other's loss exposures. Each member of the pool contributes premium based upon its loss exposures, and in exchange the pool pays for each insured's covered losses.

Pools can be formed to cover various types of loss exposures and are well-suited for organizations that are too small to use a captive insurer. The pool achieves savings through economies of scale in administration, claim handling, and the purchase of excess insurance or reinsurance.

1. Pay for Losses	O	Because, ultimately, the pool must pay for its own losses
2. Manage the Cost of Risk	O	Through economies of scale in administration
3. Manage Cash Flow Variability	O	Through risk sharing with other members
4. Maintain an Appropriate Level of Liquidity	△	If adequately funded and managed
5. Comply With Legal Requirements	△	If organized and managed within state regulations

11.f. Hold-Harmless Agreement

A contractual provision that obligates one of the parties to assume the legal liability of another party.

A hold-harmless agreement is used to assign the responsibility for losses arising from a particular relationship or activity. An illustration is an organization's agreement to assume the liability losses that may arise from the using of equipment rented from the equipment's owner.

1. Pay for Losses	△	Provided the loss exposures are covered by the agreement
2. Manage the Cost of Risk	△	Subject to any other contractual demands the other party requires before accepting the hold-harmless agreement
3. Manage Cash Flow Variability	△	Subject to the extent of the agreement
4. Maintain an Appropriate Level of Liquidity	O	Because the organization requires less liquidity with a hold-harmless agreement compared with retention or other alternative risk transfer (ART) measures
5. Comply With Legal Requirements	△	For loss exposures that are required to be transferred

11.g. Captive Insurers (Captive)

A subsidiary created to insure the loss exposures of its parent company as well as the parent's affiliates. Risk retention groups (RRGs), rent-a-captives, and protected cell companies (PCCs) are specialized types of group captives.

A captive obtains a capital investment by its parent(s) to pay for losses and manage operating expenses. The captive collects premiums, issues policies, invests assets, and pays covered losses.

1. Pay for Losses	△	If the captive is properly capitalized and managed
2. Manage the Cost of Risk	△	If the captive is properly capitalized and managed
3. Manage Cash Flow Variability	O	By charging level premiums to the parent(s) and by retaining earnings in the years with lower losses to pay for higher losses in other years
4. Maintain an Appropriate Level of Liquidity	△	If the captive is properly capitalized
5. Comply With Legal Requirements	△	If the captive is structured to do so

11.h. Finite Risk Plan

A risk financing plan that transfers a limited amount of risk to an insurer. A large part of the insured's premium creates a fund (experience fund) for the insured's own losses. The remaining amount of the premium is used to transfer a limited portion of the risk of loss to the insurer. The insurer usually shares a large proportion of its profit from the plan with the insured.

Such plans are often used for especially hazardous loss exposures for which insurance capacity is restricted or unavailable. The premiums are a very high percentage of the policy limits. An insured that can manage its losses receives profit sharing, including investment income, on the cash flow from the experience fund.

1. Pay for Losses	O	Because the insurer pays as losses become due; however, the insured ultimately pays for almost all of its own losses.
2. Manage the Cost of Risk	O	Because the profit-sharing feature encourages and rewards successful risk control efforts.
3. Manage Cash Flow Variability	O	Because cash flows are smoothed over multiple periods; however, large premiums may be due at the outset.
4. Maintain an Appropriate Level of Liquidity	X	No, premium payments are usually paid up front.
5. Comply With Legal Requirements	O	Because the insurer issues a policy guaranteeing that all covered claims will be paid.

11.i. Capital Market Solutions

A capital market is a financial marketplace through which bonds and other financial assets having a maturity of more than 1 year are purchased and sold. Capital market solutions include securitization, insurance securitization, hedging, and contingent capital arrangements.

Because capital market products involve significant time and expense to implement, only a few large organizations (including insurers and reinsurers) have used them to finance a variety of organization- and industry-specific risks.

1. Pay for Losses	△	Because some of the financial consequences of the losses are transferred to investors
2. Manage the Cost of Risk	X	No, capital market solutions are expensive relative to other risk financing measures
3. Manage Cash Flow Variability	O	Because some of the financial consequences of the losses are transferred to investors
4. Maintain an Appropriate Level of Liquidity	O	Because capital market solutions can reduce the necessary level of liquidity that an organization needs to maintain
5. Comply With Legal Requirements	△	If correctly structured

11.j. Self-Insurance

A form of retention under which an organization records it losses and maintains a formal system to pay for them.

Self-insurance is generally employed for high-frequency loss exposures because it is more efficient than filing many claims with an insurer. Self-insurance requires claim administration services similar to those provided by an insurer: recordkeeping, claim administration, loss reserving, litigation management, meeting regulatory requirements, and the purchase of excess coverage insurance.

1. Pay for Losses	△	If an organization carefully chooses the loss retention.
2. Manage the Cost of Risk	△	If the organization operates the administration economically.
3. Manage Cash Flow Variability	X	No, retained loss outcomes are uncertain.
4. Maintain an Appropriate Level of Liquidity	△	If the organization carefully: ① Chooses the loss retention level ② Purchases appropriate excess coverage ③ Accurately forecasts paid amount for retained losses
5. Comply With Legal Requirements	O	Yes, if an organization qualifies as a self-insurer for workers compensation and auto liability

11.k. Key Terms

Primary layer: The initial level of insurance coverage above any deductible.

Excess layer: A level of insurance coverage above the primary layer.

Excess coverage: Insurance that covers losses above an attachment point, below which there exists usually another insurance policy or a self-insured retention.

Umbrella policy: A liability policy to provide excess coverage above underlying policies and can also provide coverage not available in the underlying policies, subject to a self-insured retention.

Buffer layer: A level of excess insurance coverage between a primary layer and an umbrella policy.

Risk retention group: A group captive formed under the requirements of the Liability Risk Retention Act of 1986 to insure the parent organizations.

Rent-a-captive: An arrangement under which an organization rents capital from a captive to which it pays premiums and receives reimbursement for its losses.

Protected cell company (PCC): A corporate entity broken into cells so that each participating company owns an entire cell but only a portion of the overall company.

Loss limit: The level at which a loss occurrence is limited for the purpose of calculating a retrospectively rated premium.

SECTION 4. Risk Financing

Securitization: The process of creating a marketable investment security based on a financial transaction's expected cash flows.

Insurance securitization: The process of creating a marketable insurance-linked security in accordance with the cash flows that arise from the transfer of insurable risks.

Hedging: A financial transaction in which one asset is held to offset the risk associated with another asset.

Derivative: A financial contract that derives its value from the value of another asset.

Contingent capital arrangement: An agreement, created before any losses occur, that allows an organization to raise cash by selling stock or issuing debt at prearranged terms following a loss occurs that exceeds a certain threshold.

11.1. Risk Financing Measures

Which of the following statements is not true with regard to the Risk Financing Measures?

I. A hold harmless agreement is a noninsurance risk transfer measure.

II. Self-insurance is often employed to cover workers compensation and other loss exposures that have claim payouts that extend over time.

III. Self-insurance is an informal retention plan through which an organization pays losses using cash flows or current liquid assets without any method of recording losses.

IV. The premium for a finite risk insurance plan is a very high percentage of the policy limits.

V. A finite risk insurance plan typically provides lower limits than guaranteed cost insurance.

(A) I and III only

(B) III and V only

(C) II and IV only

(D) IV and V only

Answer

III. Self-insurance requires claim administration services similar to those provided by an insurer: recordkeeping, claim administration, loss reserving, litigation management, meeting regulatory requirements, and the purchase of excess coverage insurance.

V. A finite risk insurance plan typically provides higher limits than guaranteed cost insurance.

The correct answer is (B) III and V only.

11.2. Captive Insurers

Which of the following statements is true with regard to Captive Insurers?

I. Captive insurers are prohibited from underwriting loss exposures not directly related to the captive's parent or affiliates.

II. Captive insurers are used to insure property loss exposures that are difficult to insure in the primary market.

III. Captive insurers are not permitted to transfer the financial consequences of insured loss exposures to other insurers.

IV. Rent-a-captive is a group captive formed under the requirements of the Liability Risk Retention Act of 1986 to insure parent organizations.

(A) I only

(B) II only

(C) III and IV only

(D) None of the above

Answer

I. Captive insurers are not prohibited from underwriting loss exposures not directly related to the captive's parent or affiliates.

III. Captive insurers are permitted to transfer the financial consequences of insured loss exposures to other insurers through reinsurance.

IV. Rent-a-captive is an arrangement under which an organization rents capital from a captive to which it pays premiums and receives reimbursement for its losses. Risk retention group is a group captive formed under the requirements of the Liability Risk Retention Act of 1986 to insure parent organizations.

The correct answer is (B) II only.

11.3. Retrospective Rating Plans

Which of the following statements is not true with regard to Retrospective Rating Plans?

I. An organization must have a substantial insurance premium to benefit from retrospective rating.

II. Retrospective rating adjusts premiums for the current policy period based on actual losses from prior policy periods.

III. The loss limit for a retrospective rating plan is the most the insurer will pay per occurrence for a loss.

IV. Retrospective rating plans can provide financial stability if the loss limit and maximum premium are set at the proper levels.

V. If a retrospective rating plan covers more than one type of loss exposure, the insured benefits from the stability provided through diversification by retaining losses from different types of loss exposures under a single plan.

(A) I only

(B) II and III only

(C) IV and V only

(D) I and V only

Answer

II. Retrospective rating adjusts premiums for the current policy period based on actual losses from current policy period not prior policy periods.

III. The loss limit for a retrospective rating plan is the level at which a loss occurrence is limited for the purpose of calculating a retrospectively rated premium.

The correct answer is (B) II and III only.

SECTION 4. Risk Financing

SECTION 5. ENTERPRISE-WIDE RISK MANAGEMENT

Topic 12: ERM in Improving Strategic Decision Making

Topic 13: ERM for Business Uncertainties and Major RM Frameworks

Topic 12: ERM in Improving Strategic Decision Making

CPCU 500 Review Notes / Assignment 5. Enterprise-Wide Risk Management / EO 1, 2

12.a. Traditional Risk Management Versus ERM

There are four major differences between traditional RM and ERM.

	Traditional RM	ERM
1. Risk categories	Hazard risks are pure risks including property damage from perils such as fire and explosion or losses stemming from accidents and injuries to employees or customers. Operational risks are pure risks that arise out of service, processing, or manufacturing activities.	Financial risks, which include interest rate risk, competitive risk, inflation, and market-timing risks, among others. Strategic risks, which include management decisions regarding new products, emerging competitors, and planning issues
2. Strategic integration	Involves only in the elements of the organization's strategy that deal with pure risk and hazard risks.	Integrates with the entire organization's strategy and considers the global array of risks which can be represented by a three-dimensional representation of attributes (resources, events, impacts) known as the exposure spaces model.

	Traditional RM	**ERM**
3. Performance metrics	Success can be measured both as an activity and as a result.	Seeks to optimize risk taking in relationship to strategic goals. Optimization is both an situation and a process through which the organization searches for the equilibrium between risk and outcome in relationship to strategic goals
4. Organizational structure	The traditional risk manager generally reports to an organizational department such as finance, operations, or legal.	The enterprise risk manager-often known as a chief risk officer may report to the CEO or the board of directors and work as both a facilitator of and an educator about the ERM process. The chief risk officer helps the enterprise create a risk culture in which individual department heads and project managers are referred to as "risk owners."

12.b. Improving Strategic Decision Making With ERM

An organization that incorporates ERM into its strategic planning process improves its decision making in several ways, including these: ① It can address potentially devastating threats. ② It can exploit opportunities by incorporating them into its current business model or completely reinventing a new model that will successfully carry it into the future. ③ It can use ERM as a process to manage unwanted variations from expectations.

12.c. Integrating ERM and Strategic Planning

To integrate ERM, an organization's executives can follow this process:

1. Develop ERM goals	ERM goals include considerations regarding ① the organization's risk appetite, ② why the organization is establishing the ERM program, ③ the business or organizational need for an ERM program, ④ the intended scope of the ERM program, ⑤ how ERM will assist the organization in meeting its strategic goals, ⑥ how the organization defines ERM, ⑦ whether the organization has a function- or department focused culture or a collaborative culture, and how that will affect ERM implementation.
2. Risk Assessment	An organization's board and executives assess risks to identify threats that can undermine the organization and to identify opportunities that can benefit the organization. These risks involve changes in competition, customers, technology, the economy, politics, and regulation. After risks to strategy are identified, the "criticality" of the risk to the organization is determined so that the organization can prioritize risks for treatment.

3. Risk Treatment	Possible treatments for risks to an organization's strategy include some traditional risk management treatments, such as avoidance and transfer. Additional treatments are applied in ERM: ① Accept: Accept the risk by planning for ways to deal with the uncertainty if it occurs. ② Mitigate: Initiate activities to reduce the probability, impact, or timing of a risk event to an acceptable risk tolerance. ③ Optimize/exploit: Develop actions to optimize positive consequences to achieve gains.
4. Monitor and Review	Risks to strategy are monitored by trends, triggering events, and warning signs that were identified during the assessment phase for each risk identified. Information will come from a variety of sources, such as newsletters, regulatory announcements, and surveys.

12.1. Enterprise-Wide Risk Management

Which of the following statements is not true with regard to Enterprise-Wide Risk Management?

I. ERM emphasizes the interrelationships between pure and speculative risk.

II. The chief risk officer helps the enterprise create a risk culture in which individual department heads and project managers are identified as risk owners.

III. Enterprise-wide risk management (ERM) considers the global array of risks that affect an organization, which can be represented by a three-dimensional depiction of attributes. These attributes are resources, events, and impacts.

IV. A wholesale grocer is evaluating the introduction of a fleet safety program to reduce both worker injuries and liability claims arising from its extensive over-the-road exposure. The grocer would consider potential to invest savings in growth opportunities under an ERM framework, but generally not under a traditional risk management (RM) framework.

V. The iterative aspect of ERM is that the risk management process is engaged to identify and manage each discoverable risk. The recursive aspect of ERM is that the risk management process is revisited on a regular basis to maintain its optimization in relationship to strategic goals.

(A) I only

(B) II and III only

(C) IV and V only

(D) None of the above

Answer

The correct answer is (D) none of the above.

12.2. Enterprise-Wide Risk Management

Which of the following statements is true with regard to Enterprise-Wide Risk Management?

I.   While identifying risks to strategy using the enterprise-wide risk management process, an organization might ask the question, "What if an event occurs that decreases the product yield for one of our major competitors"? If the likelihood of the event is high, accept would be the most appropriate to treat this risk.

II. Risk professional Adam has assigned a high likelihood to the risk that a competitor will cut prices in the market in which his organization operates. In analyzing this potential risk, Adam decides that if this threat materializes, his organization's strategy will be to launch a marketing campaign that emphasizes his firm's superior product features, so at to reduce the risk to an acceptable level. This is an example of optimize for treating risks to strategy.

III. One way the ERM process enhances the risk management process is by adding a decision step prior to risk treatment that asks the risk manager to determine whether residual impact is within risk tolerance/appetite.

IV.

(A) I only

(B) II only

(C) III only

(D) None of the above

Answer

I. If the likelihood of the event that decreases the product yield for one of our major competitors is high, optimize/exploit would be the most appropriate to treat this risk.

II. This is an example of mitigate for treating risks to strategy.

The correct answer is (C) III only.

Topic 13: ERM for Business Uncertainties and RM Frameworks

CPCU 500 Review Notes / Assignment 5. Enterprise-Wide Risk Management / EO 3, 4

13.a. ERM in Approaching Business Uncertainties

An organization that has adopted an enterprise-wide risk management (ERM) approach monitors risks, threats, and opportunities that arise from many sources. This approach provides two important benefits: ① enhanced decision making and ② improved risk communication.

13.b. Enhanced Decision Making with ERM

An ERM approach allows an organization to systematically explore new opportunities for economic efficiencies while managing threats that stem from internal and external contexts.

Increased Profitability (Economic Efficiency)	When an organization adopts an ERM approach, unexpected occurrences or variations cause much less disruption because the organization has already incorporated the possibility of such occurrences or variations into its decision-making process, allowing it to increase its profitability.
Reduced Volatility	ERM provides a systematic framework that allows organizations to deploy capital through organization-wide decision making, which ultimately results in stable earnings projections to fund future projects.
Improved Ability to Meet Strategic Goals	ERM can minimize variation through thorough risk identification and assessment, thus improving the organization's ability to meet its strategic goals.
Increased Management Accountability	The board and senior executives establish the organization's overall mission, vision, and strategic goals, but each manager is responsible and accountable for decision making about risks within his or her individual unit.

13.c. Improved Risk Communication with ERM

ERM also encourages an organization to widely communicate its risk management approach across all of its layers. This includes making all managers aware of the need to identify obstacles that could interfere with achievement of the organization's strategic goals.

Management consensus	ERM improves management consensus by creating a corporate culture that embraces risk as an additional component of each decision. By empowering all managers to consider risk optimization and the cost of risk, ERM provides them with complete information about the potential effects of a decision, including its downsides and upsides.
Stakeholder acceptance	ERM improves acceptance by internal stakeholders by building a spirit of cooperation among management. Managers will build an understanding that the way they manage risk will have a positive impact on the organization, which, in turn, will benefit them personally.

13.d. Major Risk Management Frameworks and Standards

Compliance with standards, even those that generally are not compulsory or certifiable, such as ERM standards, demonstrates that an organization is following best practices.

ISO 31000:2009	ISO 31000:2009 is a publication issued by the International Organization for Standardization. ISO 31000:2009 provides an international standard for risk management as well as a generic approach to risk management applicable within any industry sector.
BS 31100	In 2008, the British Standards Institution (BSI) published British Standard (BS) 31100 as a code of practice for risk management.
COSO II	The Committee of Sponsoring Organizations of the Treadway Commission (COSO) published the COSO Enterprise Risk Management-Integrated Framework (known as COSO II or COSO ERM) in 2004.
AS/NZS 4360	Risk Management, a joint Australian/New Zealand Standard for ERM known as AS/NZS 4360, was published in 2004 as a generic framework for managing risk.

FERMA	The Federation of European Risk Management Associations (FERMA) consists of the national risk management associations, individual risk managers from Central European countries, and representatives from health organizations, educational sectors, and public sectors.
Basel II	Basel II was issued by the Basel Committee on Banking Supervision in 2004 to provide recommendations on banking laws and regulations. It establishes risk and capital management rules designed to ensure that a bank holds capital reserves appropriate to the risk the bank exposes itself to through its lending and investment practices.
Solvency II	Solvency II, developed by the European Commission in 2007 (sometimes referred to as "Basel II for insurers"), consists of regulatory requirements for insurance firms that operate in the European Union. It facilitated the development of a single market in insurance services in Europe while providing adequate consumer protection.

13.1. ERM in Approaching Business Uncertainties

Which of the following statements is not true with regard to ERM in Approaching Business Uncertainties?

I. An organization that has adopted an enterprise-wide risk management approach monitors risks, threats, and opportunities that arise from a variety of sources. The two important benefits provided by this approach verses traditional risk management are improved risk communication and enhanced decision making.

II. The focus in a strong ERM program is on monitoring systemic risks inherent in the organization that can adversely affect quarterly profits and losses.

III. A strong ERM program encourages the buy-in of an organization's stakeholders by establishing management strategies that protect the organization's reputation and assets.

IV. If an organization builds supply chain resilience into its operational model, it demonstrates the use of an ERM approach improving decisions and promoting economic efficiency.

(A) I only

(B) II only

(C) II and III only

(D) IV only

Answer

II. An organization that adopts an ERM approach monitors systemic risks inherent in the organization that can adversely affect its long-term financial outlook, not just quarterly profits and losses.

The correct answer is (B) II only.

13.2. Major Risk Management Frameworks and Standards

Which of the following statements is not true with regard to the Major Risk Management Frameworks and Standards?

I. The Committee of Sponsoring Organizations of the Treadway Commission (COSO) published what is referred to as COSO II. COSO II, a risk management framework, focuses on threats to the organization and application of controls.

II. A purpose of Basel II is to promote confidence in the financial stability of the insurance sector.

III. ISO 31000:2009 provides an international standard for risk management as well as a generic approach to risk management applicable within any industry sector.

IV. A purpose of Solvency II is to ensure that capital allocation is more risk sensitive.

V. AS/NZS 4360 is intended to provide only a broad overview of risk management. Organizations are expected to interpret this guide in the context of their own environments and to develop their own specific ERM approaches.

(A) I and III only

(B) II only

(C) II and IV only

(D) V only

Answer

II. A purpose of Basel II is to promote confidence in the financial stability of the banking sector.

The correct answer is (B) II only.

SECTION 5. Enterprise-Wide Risk Management

SECTION 6. INSURANCE AS A RISK MANAGEMENT TECHNIQUE

Topic 14: Benefits of Insurance and Government Insurance Programs

Topic 15: Ideally Insurable Loss Exposures

Topic 14: Benefits of Insurance and Government Insurance Programs

CPCU 500 Review Notes / Assignment 6. Insurance as a Risk Management Technique / EO 1, 2, 6

14.a. Pooling

Pooling arrangements function best (reduce the most risk to the group) if the loss exposures being pooled are independent of (uncorrelated with) each other.

Losses are independent if a loss at one loss exposure has no impact on the probability of a loss at another loss exposure. Correlated loss exposures (exposures which are not independent) can nevertheless benefit from pooling arrangements, so long as the loss exposures are not perfectly positively correlated (that is, if a loss happens to one exposure, it definitely happens to the other).

14.b. How Pooling Reduces Risk

A pooling arrangement benefits society mainly because it decreases the variability for the cost of loss for each individual in the pool. As the number of members of the pool increases, the standard deviation per member continuously decrease.

Pooling arrangements do not prevent losses or transfer risk; they reduce each individual's risk or uncertainty through sharing of losses and resources.

14.c. How Insurance Uses Pooling

Although an insurer resembles a formal pooling mechanism, there are two key differences between pooling and insurance. ① Pooling is a risk-sharing mechanism, whereas insurance is primarily a risk transfer mechanism. The insurance contract transfers the risk from the insured to the insurer in exchange for premiums. ② The insurer has additional financial resources that enable it to provide a stronger guarantee that sufficient funds will be available in the event of a loss, further reducing risk. Additional financial resources are primarily derived from these sources: Initial capital from investors; Retained earnings.

14.d. Benefits of Insurance

Pay for losses	The primary role of insurance is to indemnify (restore to pre-loss status) individuals and organizations for covered losses. A factory that burns is rebuilt, restoring employment to the workers and a revenue stream to the investors.
Manage cash flow uncertainty	Insurance provides financial compensation when covered losses occur. Therefore, insurance greatly reduces the uncertainty created by many loss exposures. A family is able to purchase a home with the assurance that their homeowners policy will compensate them for their investment if a loss occurs.
Comply with legal requirements	Insurance can be used both to meet the statutory and contractual requirements of insurance coverage and to provide evidence of financial resources. A car owner purchases automobile insurance to meet state financial responsibility requirements.
Promote risk control activity	Insurance policies may provide insureds with incentives to undertake loss control activities as a result of policy requirements or premium savings incentives. Insurance premiums on an office building are reduced when a sprinkler system is installed

Efficient use of insured's resources	Insurance makes it unnecessary to set aside a large amount of money to pay for the financial consequences of risk exposures that can be insured. This allows that money to be used more.
	A business owner is able to use capital to make investments in equipment rather than holding money in reserve for losses that might occur.
Support for insured's credit	Insurance facilitates loans to individuals and organizations by guaranteeing that the lender will be paid if the collateral for the loan (such as a house or a commercial building) is destroyed or damaged by an insured event, thereby reducing the lender's uncertainty.
	An investment group obtains a loan for the construction of an apartment building. The insurance policy names the mortgage company, which will be compensated to the extent of loan value in the event of a loss.
Source of investment funds	The timing of insurer's cash flows, premiums collected up front, and claims paid at a later date enable insurers to invest funds in a variety of investment vehicles.
	An insurance company invests in municipal bonds for the construction of community schools and public buildings, which supports job growth and community involvement.
Reduce social burden	Insurance helps reduce the burden of uncompensated accident victims to society.
	A family breadwinner injured in an auto accident is compensated for lost wages by the insurance company rather than by unemployment compensation or other social welfare programs.

14.e. Rationale for Government Involvement

Rationale for Government Involvement In addition to market failures, other reasons for government involvement in insurance include these:

To fill insurance needs unmet by private insurers	When private insurers are unable or unwilling to satisfy certain insurance needs, government programs can provide insurance to meet legitimate public demands
To compel people to buy a particular type of insurance	Federal and state governments are involved in insurance to facilitate compulsory insurance purchases.
To obtain greater efficiency and/or provide convenience to insurance buyers	By reducing either the time or the resources insurance buyers need to obtain the desired insurance coverage, adds to the efficiency of the market.
To achieve collateral social purposes	By making use of the pooling mechanism, insurance can reduce risk to society. This is beneficial both to society and to the overall economy.

14.f. Level of Government Involvement

Exclusive insurer	The government can be an exclusive insurer either because of law or because no private insurer offers a competing plan. This involvement can be as a primary insurer or as a reinsurer.
Partner with private insurers	Government partnerships with private insurers can develop when private insurers are no longer able to adequately provide coverages they had typically offered previously.
Competitor to private insurers	This type of involvement often evolves when the private insurance market has not failed but is not operating as efficiently as regulators would like.

14.g. Federal Compared With State Programs

In the event the rationale for government involvement extends beyond state boundaries or would affect interstate commerce, the federal government should be running the insurance program.

Good examples of property-liability federal insurance programs are the National Flood Insurance Program, the Terrorism Risk Insurance Program, and Federal Crop Insurance.

Examples of property-liability insurance provided by state governments are workers compensation insurance, beach and windstorm plans, and residual auto plans.

14.1. Pooling

Which of the following statements is true with regard to Pooling?

I. Pooling arrangements combine the loss exposures and funds of pool members with the intention of sharing losses.

II. Pooling arrangements reduce the most risk if the loss exposures being pooled are correlated.

III. Generally, a loss to one member of a pooling arrangement increases the probability of a loss to another member.

IV. As the number of members within a pool increases, on a per member basis the expected value of losses continues to decrease.

V. Lyon and Peney are both equally good drivers with clean records, and they drive similar cars. After they marry, Peney adds Lyon to her personal auto policy and cancels his old policy. Since Lyon has been added onto Peney's policy, the potential loss severity of an accident involving Peney's car is unchanged.

(A) I and II only

(B) II and III only

(C) II and IV only

(D) I and V only

Answer

II. Pooling arrangements reduce the most risk to the group when the loss exposures being pooled are independent of (uncorrelated with) one another.

III. Losses are independent when a loss at one loss exposure has no effect on the probability of a loss at another loss exposure.

IV. As the number of members in a pool increases, on a per member basis the expected value of losses remains unchanged. As the number of members of the pool increases, the standard deviation per member continues to decrease. Pooling arrangements do not prevent losses or transfer risk; they reduce each individual's risk or uncertainty through sharing of losses and resources.

The correct answer is (D) I and V only.

14.2. Pooling

Which of the following statements is not true with regard to the below situation?

The Magnus Bus Company is a publicly held corporation providing bus for school transportation to private and public schools in Midland County. Magnus owns 200 school buses, garaged in three different cities in the county. Its major competitors are two larger bus companies that operate in the same general area. School districts and private schools generally award contracts towards the lowest bidder from among the bus companies, but they also consider general performance and level of service in their evaluations. Suppose Magnus were to get into a formal arrangement with the Green Bus Company, a similar company that is operating in another state, to pool the losses suffered by both companies.

(A) An example of a correlated loss exposure is a bus breakdown caused by a defective design in Magnus's buses.

(B) Another example of a correlated loss exposure is a serious bus accident resulting in multiple deaths.

(C) Assuming both Magnus's and Green's fleets included buses with the same defect (perfectly positively correlated loss), with the arrangement with Green, the Magnus's risks would be unchanged. If losses are not perfectly positively correlated, some risk could be reduced through pooling, although the magnitude is less than with uncorrelated losses.

(D) With the arrangement with Green, although the number of serious accidents for which Magnus would be required to share resources with Green would increase, Magnus's share of the losses would become more predictable, reducing Magnus's risks.

Answer

(B) An example of an uncorrelated loss exposure is a serious bus accident resulting in multiple deaths.

The correct answer is (B)

14.3. Benefits of Insurance

Which of the following statements is not true with regard to Benefits of Insurance?

I. The primary role of insurance is to indemnify individuals and organizations for covered losses.

II. One disadvantage of insurance is that it promotes inefficient use of policyholders' funds.

III. Insurance provides a source of investment funds for insurers, but not for insureds.

IV. Investment income helps keep insurance premiums at a reasonable level.

V. Insurance helps reduce the financial burden to society by compensating accident victims.

(A) I and II only

(B) II and III only

(C) III and IV only

(D) I and V only

Answer

II, III. Insurance makes it unnecessary to set aside a large amount of money to pay for the financial consequences of risk exposures that can be insured. This allows that money to be used more. A business owner is able to use capital to make investments in equipment rather than holding money in reserve for losses that might occur.

The correct answer is (B) II and III only.

14.4. Benefits of Insurance

Which of the following statements is not true with regard to Benefits of Insurance?

I.   Two individuals each have a 70% probability of not suffering a homeowners loss in a given year. Assuming that losses involving these two homes are independent of one another, and that the two individuals enter into a pooling arrangement, the probability of neither individual suffering a loss is 49%.

II. As a single mother on a very tight budget, Jennifer is tempted to skimp on her insurance. However, her friend Mehmet tells her not to skimp on insurance, because it will help manage her cash flows. Mehmet's point is that when her car's windshield breaks, Jennifer has to pay only $50 of the $900 cost of replacing it.

III. Hyundai Construction Company pays less than its competitors for workers compensation insurance because Hyundai has had substantially fewer employee injuries than other firms in its class. This illustrates enable efficient use of resources among benefits of insurance.

IV.

  (A) I only

  (B) II and III only

  (C) III only

  (D) None of the above

Answer

III. This illustrates promote risk control among benefits of insurance.

The correct answer is (C) III only.

14.5. Government Insurance Programs

Which of the following statements is true with regard to Government Insurance Programs?

I.   Government insurers cannot function as primary insurers for duties such as collecting premiums, providing coverage, or paying claims.

II. Government programs can operate as reinsurers, reinsuring 100 percent of the risk or that part in excess of the private insurer's retention.

III. Businesses seeking flood insurance under the National Flood Insurance Program (NFIP) must purchase it at local federal government offices.

IV. Various state insurance programs provide crop insurance for perils such as drought, disease, excessive rain and hail.

(A) I only

(B) II only

(C) II and III only

(D) III and IV only

Answer

I. Government insurers can collect premiums, provide coverage, or pay claims as like primary insurers.

III. Businesses seeking flood insurance under the NFIP could purchase it through a private insurer.

IV. Federal Crop Insurance programs provide crop insurance for perils such as drought, disease, excessive rain and hail.

The correct answer is (B) II only.

14.6. Government Insurance Programs

Which of the following statements is not true with regard to Government Insurance Programs?

I.   Government partnerships with private insurers usually develop in especially desirable lines of business.

II. Government insurance programs can operate in direct competition with private insurers.

III. Fair Access to Insurance Requirements (FAIR) plans make basic property insurance available to property owners who can't get it otherwise.

IV. The state government provides workers compensation insurance to employers who cannot get it from private insurers.

V.   Following the terrorist attacks on the United States, insurers became reluctant to provide property insurance on target properties until the federal Terrorism Risk Insurance Program (TRIP) was introduced. The social purpose of this program is to prevent economic disruption.

(A) I only

(B) II only

(C) III and IV only

(D) V only

Answer

I. Government partnerships with private insurers can develop when private insurers are no longer able to adequately provide coverages they had typically offered previously.

The correct answer is (A) I only.

Topic 15: Ideally Insurable Loss Exposures

CPCU 500 Review Notes / Assignment 6. Insurance as a Risk Management Technique / EO 3, 4, 5

15.a. Six Characteristics of an Ideally Insurable Loss Exposure

1. Pure risk Insurable risk should be pure risks, not speculative risks	Insurance is not created to finance speculative risks. It should indemnify the insured for loss, not allow the insured to profit from the loss. Pricing insurance coverage for speculative risks would be much more complex than pricing pure risks.
2. Fortuitous losses Insurable risk should have a chance occurrence of loss from the insured's standpoint.	In the event the insured has some control over whether or when a loss will occur, the insurer is at a disadvantage for the reason that insured may have a motivation to cause a loss. Payment for intentional losses could ruin the pricing structure for insurance and increase insurance premiums for all policyholders.
3. Definite and measurable Insurable risk should be definite in time, cause, and location; and measurable.	In case a loss cannot be defined in time or measured, it would be extremely difficult for an insurer to write an insurance policy that specifies what claims to pay and how much to pay for them. At a minimum, the expenses of adjusting losses would increase and the likelihood of litigation would be greatly increased.

4. Large number of similar exposures units Insurable risk should be one of a large number of similar exposures units	A large pool of similar exposure units enables the insurer to more accurately project losses and determine appropriate premiums because loss statistics can be maintained over time and losses for similar exposure units can be projected with a higher degree of accuracy.
5. Independent and not catastrophic Insurable risk should not be subject to a loss that would simultaneously affect many other similar loss exposures	For insurers to make use of pooling most effectively, the insured exposure units must be independent. When a large number of insureds who are covered for the same type of loss were to incur losses simultaneously, the insurance mechanism would not operate economically and losses to insurer could be catastrophic.
6. Affordable Insurable risk should have premiums that are economically feasible.	Demand and supply of insurance show that if an insurer cannot provide the insurance product at a reasonable premium, there will be no demand. To maintain the balance of demand and supply, the insurance mechanism must establish a pricing structure that adequately supports the expenses for providing coverage at a price (premium) appropriate for the purchaser when compared to the potential loss.

15.b. Ideally Insurable Characteristics: Property Loss Exposures

	Commercial Property		Personal Property	
	Fire	Wind or Flood	Fire	Wind or Flood
1. Pure risk	Yes, except arson for profit	Yes	Yes, except arson for profit	Yes
2. Fortuitous losses	Yes, except arson for profit	Yes	Yes, except arson for profit	Yes
3. Definite and measurable	Yes	Yes	Yes	Yes
4. Large number of similar exposures units	① Depends on property location, type, and use	① Depends on property location, type, and use	Yes	Yes
5. Independent and not catastrophic	Yes	② Can be catastrophic	Yes	② Can be catastrophic
6. Affordable	Yes	③ Depends on location	Yes	③ Depends on location

① Some commercial properties are unique and might not be part of a large number of similar exposure units.

② Multiple locations may be subject to the same catastrophic loss.

③ In areas subject to catastrophic losses, economical premiums might not be possible.

15.c. Ideally Insurable Characteristics: Liability Loss Exposures

	Commercial Liability		Personal Liability	
	Premises and operations liability	Products liability	Premises liability	Automobiles liability
1. Pure risk	Yes	Yes	Yes	Yes
2. Fortuitous losses	Yes	Yes	Yes	Yes
3. Definite and measurable	Yes	① Depends on product	Yes	Yes
4. Large number of similar exposures units	Yes	Depends on product	Yes	Yes
5. Independent and not catastrophic	Yes	② Depends on product	Yes	Yes
6. Affordable	Yes	③ Depends on product	Yes	Yes

① For products liability, causes of injury are not always definite, and losses may be difficult to measure in monetary terms.

② A products liability loss could be catastrophic if the product is widely distributed and many claims result from a loss.

③ For inherently dangerous products, economical premiums may not be feasible.

15.d. Ideally Insurable Characteristics: Net Income Loss Exposures

	Commercial Net Income		Personal Net Income
	Loss with property losses	Loss with liability losses	Unemployment
1. Pure risk	Yes	Yes	Yes
2. Fortuitous losses	Yes	Yes	Depends on person involved
3. Definite and measurable	Yes	② May not be definite	Yes
4. Large number of similar exposures units	Yes	Yes	Yes
5. Independent and not catastrophic	① May be catastrophic	Yes	Yes
6. Affordable	Depends on location	Yes	Yes

① Net income losses associated with property losses can exhibit ideally insurable characteristics with the exception that they may be catastrophic.

② Net income losses associated with liability losses can exhibit ideally insurable characteristics except that they may not be definite in time, because there is no specific time when losses to net income cease. For example, lost reputation or marketability after a liability loss may continue long after claims are settled.

15.e. Ideally Insurable Characteristics: Personnel

	Commercial Personnel	
	Death	Retirement
1. Pure risk	Yes	Yes
2. Fortuitous losses	Yes	Depends on circumstances and personnel involved
3. Definite and measurable	① Depends on personnel involved	① Depends on personnel involved
4. Large number of similar exposures units	② Depends on personnel involved	② Depends on personnel involved
5. Independent and not catastrophic	Yes	Yes
6. Affordable	Yes	Yes

① The cost of loss of a key employee through death or retirement may be difficult to measure.

② The potential loss of key employees does not usually involve large numbers of similar exposure units.

15.f. Ideally Insurable Characteristics: Life, Health, Retirement

	Personal Life, Health, Retirement		
	Life loss exposure	Health loss exposure	Retirement loss exposure
1. Pure risk	Yes	Yes	Yes
2. Fortuitous losses	Yes, except for suicide	① Depends on cause of loss	② Not usually, but may be forced
3. Definite and measurable	Yes	Depends on cause of loss	Yes
4. Large number of similar exposures units	Yes	Yes	Yes
5. Independent and not catastrophic	Yes	Yes	Yes
6. Affordable	Usually	Usually	N/A

① Health insurance is subject to moral and morale hazards because many causes of loss to health are under some control of the individual involved.

② Retirement does not usually exhibit the fortuitous characteristic of ideally insurable loss exposures because the individual has control over savings and choice of retirement dates.

15.1. Ideally Insurable Loss Exposures

Which of the following statements is not true with regard to Ideally Insurable Loss Exposures?

I.   In case losses are not fortuitous, the insurer cannot calculate a proper premium.

II. A typical function that insurance provides is a spreading of risk across a large number of similar exposure units in the same period.

III. An unidentified vandal spray-paints graffiti on the insured's garage is an illustration of a fortuitous loss.

IV. Loss exposures such as homes and automobiles generally will not satisfy the ideally insurable requirement that the exposure be of a large number of similar exposure units.

V.   Of all the so-called characteristics of an ideally insurable loss exposure, probably the most important is that the insurer is able to charge a premium that the insured can afford to pay.

  (A) I and II only

  (B) III only

  (C) IV only

  (D) IV and V only

Answer

IV. Loss exposures such as homes and automobiles generally meet the ideally insurable requirement that the exposure be of a large number of similar exposure units.

The correct answer is (C) IV only.

15.2. Ideally Insurable Loss Exposures

Which of the following statements is not true with regard to Ideally Insurable Loss Exposures?

I.   For any loss exposure to be ideally insurable it must be definite in time, cause, and location.

II. Indemnification is the procedure of restoring an insured to a pre-loss financial condition.

III. In case a loss exposure includes the possibility of gain, it is a more attractive risk to insure.

IV. Commercial general liability insurance policies written on an occurrence basis apply to bodily injury and property damage that occurs during the policy period. This provision supports the principle that insurable loss exposures must, ideally, be fortuitous.

V.   Private insurers are often unwilling to provide windstorm insurance on coastal properties. This is because the loss exposures fail to meet the criterion that ideally insurable exposures must be independent and not catastrophic.

(A) I and II only

(B) III only

(C) III and IV only

(D) IV and V only

Answer

III. Insurable risk should be pure risks, not speculative risks

IV. This provision supports the principle that insurable loss exposures must, ideally, be definite.

The correct answer is (C) III and IV only.

15.3. Insurability of Commercial Loss Exposures

Which of the following statements is true with regard to Insurability of Commercial Loss Exposures?

I. Retirement as a personnel loss insurance is generally available to compensate organizations for the resulting loss when key employees retire.

II. Because retirement is usually planned, most resulting personnel losses can be handled with proper planning.

III. The personnel loss associated with retirement is the value of any pension or other benefits paid, which is easily measured.

IV. Net income losses caused by the business environment represent pure risk.

V. Net income losses resulting from liability losses are measurable because the timing and duration of the loss are definite.

(A) I only

(B) II only

(C) III and IV only

(D) IV and V only

Answer

I, III. The cost of loss of a key employee through death or retirement may be difficult to measure. The potential loss of key employees does not usually involve large numbers of similar exposure units. Therefore, it is generally not available to compensate organizations for the resulting loss when key employees retire.

IV. Net income losses caused by the business environment do not meet the first characteristic of the loss exposures involving pure risk.

V. Net income losses associated with liability losses can exhibit ideally insurable characteristics except that they may not be definite in time, because there is no specific time when losses to net income cease. For example, lost reputation or marketability after a liability loss may continue long after claims are settled.

The correct answer is (B) II only.

15.4. Insurability of Commercial Loss Exposures

Which of the following statements is not true with regard to Insurability of Commercial Loss Exposures?

I.   Net income losses resulting from liability losses are insured by a variety of business income coverages.

II. Net income loss exposures associated with property losses exhibit almost all the characteristics of ideally insurable risks.

III. Samsung Corporation wishes to purchase key person life insurance to provide a financial cushion against the loss of its chief executive officer. This personnel loss exposure for Samsung meets all of the following characteristics of an ideally insurable loss exposure, except definite and measurable.

IV. Lotte Meat Company, which provides beef products to supermarkets nationwide, faces the possibility of a contamination problem that could generate claims from many consumers of its products. Although Lotte is eager to purchase products liability insurance, insurers are reluctant to provide it because the number of claims resulting from a single loss could be catastrophic.

(A) I only

(B) I and II only

(C) III only

(D) III and IV only

Answer

I. Net income losses resulting from property losses, not liability losses, are insured by a variety of business income coverages.

The correct answer is (A) I only.

15.5. Insurability of Personal Loss Exposures

Which of the following statements is not true with regard to Insurability of Personal Loss Exposures?

I.   Homes can be grouped into classes that face essentially the same loss potential.

II. Commercial property exposures are easier to group into classes than individual homes.

III. Automobile liability loss exposures meet all of the characteristics of ideally insurable personal loss exposures.

IV. When insuring homes, insurers need not avoid excessive concentration of loss exposures.

V.   Residential property loss exposures associated with fire, windstorm, and flood involve a large number of similar exposure units.

  (A) I and II only

  (B) I and III only

  (C) II and IV only

  (D) II and V only

Answer

II. Individual homes are easier to group into classes than commercial property exposures.

VI. Insurers must avoid homeowners with arson-for-profit motives and concentrations of homes in areas subject to catastrophic losses, which may not be economically feasible to insure.

The correct answer is (C) II and IV only.

15.6. Ideally Insurable Loss Exposures

Which of the following statements is not true with regard to Ideally Insurable Loss Exposures?

Ayala Mall is a mall of sixty retail stores located along the Outer Banks of North Carolina's shoreline. Outer Banks Insurance Company, a small local property insurer that insures more than 40 percent of properties in the Outer Banks area, is considering selling a commercial property policy to Ayala Mall that includes coverage for windstorm damage.

I. Ayala Mall does meet the first three characteristics for windstorm damage. Windstorm is a pure risk, fortuitous, and definite and measurable.

II. Because the mall is a retail mall, it probably does meet the fourth characteristic of being a large number of similar exposure units.

III. From Outer Banks Insurance Company's perspective, the windstorm cause of loss is probably not independent and catastrophic.

IV. Outer Banks Insurance has insured a large percentage of the local market, and a major hurricane would affect a large percentage of its insureds. This may make it difficult for Outer Banks Insurance to charge a feasible premium and still maintain its claim paying ability.

(A) I only

(B) III only

(C) II and IV only

(D) None of the above

Answer

The correct answer is (D) none of the above.

SECTION 6. Insurance as a Risk Management Technique

.

SECTION 7. INSURANCE POLICY ANALYSIS

Topic 16: Characteristics and Structure of Insurance Policies

Topic 17: Policy Provisions and Analysis

Topic 16: Characteristics and Structure of Insurance Policies

CPCU 500 Review Notes / Assignment 7. Insurance Policy Analysis / EO 1, 2

16.a. Characteristics of Insurance Policies

Indemnity	An insurance policy is a contract of indemnity: a contract where the insurer agrees, in the case of a covered loss, to pay an amount directly related to the amount of the loss. The insured should be "made whole" but should not make a profit.
	An insurance policy does not always pay the full amount necessary to indemnify an insured due to policy limits, deductibles, and other policy limitations. Insurance policies may not indemnify the insured for the inconvenience, time, or any other nonfinancial expenses associated with recovering from an insured loss. Some valued policies pay a preestablished amount of money in the case of an insured loss which may be more or less compared to value of an insured loss.
Utmost good faith	Ideally, insurance contracts involve transactions of utmost good faith, in which parties act with complete honesty and disclose all relevant facts. Insureds must provide information without concealment or misrepresentation, and insurers must fulfill promises as outlined in the contract.
	A typical violation of this characteristic is fraud and/or buildup in insurance claims filed by the insured. Fraud is the misrepresentation of critical facts of a claim. Buildup is the intentional inflation of an otherwise legitimate claim.

Fortuitous losses	Insurance contracts pay for losses that are fortuitous (accidental or unexpected) from the insured's standpoint.
	Not every fortuitous losses are covered by insurance, because they are excluded by the policies.
	Many finite risk insurance contracts cover losses that have occurred but have not been settled.
Contract of adhesion	Insurance policies normally involve virtually no negotiation. Generally, an insurer chooses the precise wording in the policies it offers and the insured has little choice but to accept ("adhere to") it. Courts interpret ambiguities in such insurance contracts in the insured's favor. The reasonable expectations doctrine further protects an insured when policy clauses are ambiguous.
	Unique loss exposures that require special underwriting consideration might be negotiable.
	Manuscript policies or policies with manuscript form are not contracts of adhesion.

Exchange of unequal amounts	The exchange provided by the insured (premium) and by the insurer (promise to indemnify the insured in the case of a covered loss) is unequal. Rather, an insured's premium should be corresponding to the risk it presents to the insurer.
	Finite risk insurance policies involve an exchange of amounts closer in value than other types of policies because finite risk insurance involves little or no actual risk transfer and often functions as a loan.
Conditional	Insurance policies are conditional contracts for the reason that one must perform only under certain conditions; the insurer is obligated to pay for losses only when the insured has fulfilled all of the policy conditions.
	The insurer might be ready to waive some conditions of the policy, such as requiring the policyholder to make the damaged property available for inspection. Sometimes, the insurer may pay the claim without making the inspection.
Nontransferable	An insurance policy is a contract between two parties; the insured cannot transfer the contract to a third party without the insurer's written consent.
	Maritime policies include exceptions to the nontransferable clause for changes in ownership that occur while a ship is at sea.

16.b. Indemnity

In order to reduce or avoid moral hazards associated with indemnification, an insurance policy should not do the following: ① Overindemnify the insured ② Indemnify insureds more than once per loss.

16.c. Utmost good faith

An insurance policy may be vulnerable to misrepresentation or opportunism for two reasons. These situations could affect underwriting decisions and lead to adverse selection. The concept of utmost good faith obligates all parties to act with complete honesty and to disclose all relevant facts and therefore helps prevent these situations. ① One party to a contract has information the other party does not (information asymmetry). ② The costly verification of information may lead an insurer to fail to verify information provided by the insured.

16.d. Structure of Insurance Policies

Self-Contained Policies	A self-contained policy contains, within one document, all the provisions needed to make up a complete insurance policy.
Modular Policies	A modular policy is created by combining a set of individual components, such as one or more coverage forms, one or more causes of loss forms, and one or more conditions forms.
Preprinted Forms	Most insurance policies are assembled from one or more preprinted forms, which are designed to be used by many insureds. The forms themselves are not altered or customized for each insured.
Manuscript Forms	An insurance policy that consists of several different documents, none of which by itself forms a complete policy.
Standard Forms	An insurer may use the standard forms, developed by insurance service and advisory organizations that are also used by other insurers.
Nonstandard Forms	A nonstandard form drafted or adapted by one insurer is sometimes called a company-specific or proprietary form. All manuscript forms are nonstandard forms.
Endorsements and Other Documents	① Endorsements are added to modify a basic policy form. ② Completed application ③ Insurer's bylaws ④ Insurer's rating manual ⑤ Other documents: premium notes, inspection reports, and specification sheets or operating manuals relating to safety equipment or procedures.

16.e. Advantages of Using Modular Policies

The advantages of using modular policies, relative to self-contained policies, include the following: ① Carefully designed and coordinated provisions in the various forms minimize the possibility of gaps and overlaps. ② Consistent terminology, definitions, and policy language make coverage interpretation easier for the insured. ③ Fewer forms are required to meet a wide range of needs. ④ Underwriting is simplified because much of the basic information that must be analyzed applies to all lines of insurance. ⑤ Adverse selection problems can be reduced. ⑥ Insurers often give a package discount when several coverages are included in the same policy.

16.f. Differentiate between Preprinted and Manuscript forms.

Most insurance policies are assembled from one or more preprinted forms, which are created to be used by many insureds. The forms themselves are not altered or customized for each and every insured. Preprinted standard forms are the easiest forms to judge during policy analysis because they are commonly used and more consistently interpreted by the courts and because insurance professionals usually have more experience working with these forms.

Manuscript forms are unique forms developed through negotiation between the insurer and insured. Manuscript forms are the most challenging forms to interpret because they often contain unique wording and can vary widely in their interpretation.

16.g. Endorsements and Other Related Documents

These documents may become part of an insurance policy by being attached to or referenced within the policy: ① Endorsements: Endorsements are added to modify a basic policy form. Policies in several lines of business have "standard" endorsements that are included in most of the policies written in that line. ② Completed application-In some jurisdictions, statutes require that any written application be made part of the policy for certain lines of insurance. ③ Insurer's bylaws-With certain types of policies, such as those with mutual or reciprocal insurers, the insurer's bylaws regarding rights and duties are specified in the policy. ④ Insurer's rating manual-Some policies incorporate the insurer's rating manual by referring to it in the policy language. ⑤ Other documents-Some frequently incorporated documents include premium notes, inspection reports, and specification sheets or operating manuals relating to safety equipment or procedures.

16.h. General Policy Interpretation Rules

The following two policy interpretation rules apply when an endorsement contradicts the policy to which it is attached: ① An endorsement takes precedence over any conflicting terms in the policy. ② A handwritten endorsement supersedes a computer-printed or typewritten one.

16.1. Characteristics of Insurance Policies

Which of the following statements is not true with regard to the Characteristics of Insurance Policies?

I. Common insurance contracts are contracts of adhesion.

II. Most property and liability insurance policies contain other insurance provision clauses so as to limit overindemnification.

III. State regulators are qualified for assign insurance policies from an insolvent insurer to other insurers licensed in the state.

IV. Most property and liability insurance policies contain conditions allowing insureds to transfer policies to 3rd parties without the insurer's written permission.

V. Most property and liability insurance policies contain conditions prohibiting insurers from transferring policies to other insurers without the insured's written consent.

(A) I and II only

(B) III only

(C) IV only

(D) IV and V only

Answer

IV. An insurance policy is a contract between two parties; the insured cannot transfer the contract to a third party without the insurer's written consent.

V. Most property and liability insurance policies do not contain conditions prohibiting insurers from transferring policies to other insurers without the insured's written consent.

The correct answer is (D) IV and V only.

16.2. Characteristics of Insurance Policies

Which of the following statements is not true with regard to the Characteristics of Insurance Policies?

I.   A nonstandard form is least likely to be considered a contract of adhesion.

II. The most common violations of the concept of utmost good faith in insurance policies involve buildup in insurance claims filed by insureds and/or misrepresentation of key facts.

III. When Moe Girard, purchased his home, he did not tell his insurer that he kept flammable chemicals in his basement for use in a hobby. Girard, is aware that storing the chemicals increases the potential for loss to his home. The fact that the insurer does not have this information is an example of information asymmetry.

IV. An insurer makes sure that the tangible consideration exchanged by the insured for an insurance contract is equitable by charging a premium that is directly proportional to the insured's expected losses on an actuarially sound basis.

(A) I only

(B) II and III only

(C) II and IV only

(D) II and V only

Answer

I. A manuscript policy is least likely to be considered a contract of adhesion. All manuscript forms are nonstandard forms. But, All nonstandard forms are not manuscript forms.

The correct answer is (A) I only.

16.3. Characteristics of Insurance Policies

Which of the following statements is not true with regard to the Characteristics of Insurance Policies?

I.   David Martin was bragging to his new neighbors about how little he paid for his auto insurance for his sixteen-year-old son, who has been ticketed for speeding three times in the last two months. When one neighbor asked how he was able to buy insurance for such a low premium, Martin replied that he told the insurer that his son is twenty-five years old and has a perfect driving record. The neighbor asked Martin if he thought that what he was doing was wrong. Martin responded, "No, I've been paying premiums for twenty years without a claim. I'm just getting a discount they owe me anyway." In this situation, Martin's policy fails to exhibit utmost good faith. Utmost good faith requires that a person applying for insurance make a full and fair disclosure of the risk presented by the loss exposures to be insured.

II. Swift & Company (S&C) paid $5 million at a June auction for the only known painting by Cassandra Cole, a famous nineteenth century sculptor. S&C insured the painting under a valued policy for $5.1 million with Art Insurance Company, which renewed the policy the following June. On August 1, more than fifty paintings by Cole were discovered in a storage area at a European museum. That September, a fire destroyed the wing of the S&C where the Cole painting was on display. The market value of the original Cole painting at the time of the loss was only $1 million. In this situation, valued policies can violate the principle of indemnity by underinsuring or overinsuring a particular loss exposure. In this case, Art Insurance would still pay the full $5.1 million because the policy was in force at the time of the loss and the painting was destroyed in the fire. The payment would violate the principle of indemnity.

(A) I only

(B) II only

(C) None of the above

(D) All of the above

Answer

The correct answer is (C) none of the above.

16.4. Structure of Insurance Policies

Which of the following statements is not true with regard to the Structure of Insurance Policies?

I.   In a court of law, in the course of policy analysis, a modular policy is most difficult to interpret.

II. One benefit of the use of manuscript forms is that it can be specifically drafted or selected to cover unique loss exposures.

III. An insurance policy may reference an insurer's rating manual, making the rules and rates contained in the manual part of the policy.

IV. Company LIG sells earth-moving equipment and has a substantial inventory. Their risk management professional wants to ensure that the insurance is carefully designed and has coordinated provisions in the various forms to minimize the potential of gaps and overlaps in coverage. The most suitable policy for Company LIG is a modular policy.

V.   Since manuscript forms do not have the identical history of court interpretations regarding policy analysis, substantial delays in claim adjusting or strained relations between the insured and the insurer can occur. To reduce the possibilities of such problems, most manuscript forms are adapted from wording previously developed and used in standard forms.

(A) I only

(B) II and III only

(C) IV only

(D) I and V only

Answer

I. In a court of law, during policy analysis, a manuscript policy is most difficult to interpret.

The correct answer is (A) I only.

16.5. Structure of Insurance Policies

Which of the following statements is not true with regard to the Structure of Insurance Policies?

Janet, the owner of a high-rise office complex in New York City, has been negotiating with a consortium of insurers to design a property insurance program to provide enough coverage for her multi-billion-dollar property. Janet was not satisfied with the wording of the flood exclusion on the standard form the insurers wanted to use, so she negotiated the wording of the exclusion with the insurers. While the policy was in force, Janet's property was damaged when a water tower on the roof of the building ruptured and poured millions of gallons of water through the building. Janet's insurer denied the claim based on the wording of the flood exclusion. Janet's broker told her not to worry because in court cases involving the standard flood exclusion, the courts have "always found for the insured" in similar situations.

(A) Her broker's comment that "courts always side with the insured" applies to the standard flood exclusion, which is an example of a contract of adhesion.

(B) However, Janet negotiated the wording of the flood exclusion, which makes this policy a manuscript policy.

(C) Manuscript policies, because the insured participated in determining the wording of the policy, are not generally considered contracts of adhesion. Therefore, the court's interpretation of the standard flood exclusion may not be relevant to Janet's case.

(D) The courts may not side with Janet in answering the question of coverage in this manuscript policy.

Answer

(D) The courts may or may not side with Janet in answering the question of coverage in this manuscript policy.

The correct answer is (D).

Topic 17: Policy Provisions and Analysis

CPCU 500 Review Notes / Assignment 7. Insurance Policy Analysis / EO 3, 4

17.a. Six Common Policy Provisions

The following exhibit displays the six common policy provisions, and demonstrates how these common policy provisions apply to a claim case and the actions that an insurer might take.

Mrs. Lewis calls Hanwha Insurance Company to make a claim for the total loss of her home in a fire. The claim representative will review Mrs. Lewis's policy using the following policy provisions:

Declarations	Unique information on the insured; list of forms included in policy Outline who or what is covered, and where an when coverage applies
	① The loss must be within the inception and expiration dates. ② Mrs. Lewis must be the policyholder . ③ The damaged property must be the same as the insured location. ④ Any mortgagees on the insured property will have an insurable interest in the property. ⑤ The dollar limits of coverage are the maximum that will apply to the loss. ⑥ The claim payment will be reduced by any deductible.
Definitions	Words with special meanings in policy May limit or expand coverage based on definitions of terms
	Throughout the contract, the representative will refer to the definitions for any words that appear in quotation marks (" ") to determine whether their special meaning will have any influence on the fire claim presented by Mrs. Lewis.
Insuring Agreements	Promise to make payment Outline circumstances under which the insure agrees to pay
	The representative will review the insurance agreement that applies to the property section of the policy to determine the payment or service promised by the policy with regard to Mrs. Lewis's fire claim. An insuring agreement might be a comprehensive or a limited insuring agreement.

Conditions	Qualifications on promise to make payment
	Outline steps insured needs to take to enforce policy
	The representative will review the applicable policy conditions to determine the insured's and insurer's obligations. For example: ① The insured is obligated to produce an inventory of damaged property, provide the insurer with documents, and submit to an examination under oath. ② If the insurer and the insured disagree regarding the amount of loss, an appraisal process is described. ③ Even if the fire is determined to be an arson caused by Mrs. Lewis, Hanwha's obligation to the mortgagee is described.
Exclusions	Limitations on promise to make payment
	Limit insurer's payments based on excluded persons, places, things, or actions
	The representative will review the exclusions that apply to the damaged building and contents to clarify the coverages granted by the policy.
Miscellaneous Provisions	Wide variety of provisions that may alter policy
	May limit or expand coverage based on content of provision
	The representative will review any other policy provisions that may appear in Mrs. Lewis's policy as well as Hanwha's working procedures for claim settlement to determine the standards for measuring the extent of the loss covered under the policy.

17.b. Pre-Loss Policy Analysis

Relies on scenario analysis to determine the extent of coverage (if any) the policy provides for the losses generated by a given scenario. For insureds, the main source of information used is their past loss experience. Another source of information is the insurance producer or customer service representative consulted in the insurance transaction.

One of the limitations of scenario analysis is that, as the number of possible loss scenarios is theoretically infinite, it is impossible to take into account every possibility.

17.c. Post-Loss Analysis

The primary method of post-loss policy analysis is the DICE (an acronym representing the policy provision categories: declarations, insuring agreements, conditions, and exclusions) method, which is a systematic review of all the categories of property-casualty policy provisions.

The claims adjuster would follow the steps specified in the DICE decision tree to determine whether the family's homeowners policy covered the loss: ① check the declarations to see whether anything there would preclude coverage. If not, go to the next step. ② see whether anything in the insuring agreement would preclude coverage. If not, go to the next step. ③ check the conditions to see whether anything precluded coverage and, if not, go to the next step. ④ check the exclusions and all other policy provisions not already analyzed, including the endorsements and miscellaneous provisions, to make sure that nothing would preclude coverage. If not, determine the amount payable under the policy.

17.1. Common Policy Provisions

Which of the following statements is true with regard to the Common Policy Provisions?

I.   The property casualty insurance policy provisions that indicate who or what is covered, and where and when coverage applies, are found in the declarations.

II. The numbers and edition dates of all attached forms and endorsements are found in the policy declarations.

III. Insurance policy rating information and policy premium are found in the policy miscellaneous provisions.

IV. Auto insured Tom was surprised when he was invited to his mutual auto insurer's election of its board of directors. Tom would most likely find information relating to this type of election, in his policy's conditions.

V.   Insuring agreements in insurance policies generally serve as outline steps the insured needs to take to enforce coverage.

(A) I and II only

(B) III only

(C) III and IV only

(D) IV only

Answer

III. Insurance policy rating information and policy premium are found in the policy declarations.

IV. Tom would most likely find information relating to this type of election, in his policy's miscellaneous provisions.

V. Conditions in insurance policies generally serve as outline steps the insured needs to take to enforce coverage.

The correct answer is (A) I and II only.

17.2. Policy Analysis

Which of the following statements is not true with regard to the Policy Analysis?

I.   To figure out the extent of coverage a policy provides, pre-loss policy analysis almost exclusively uses scenario analysis.

II. For most insureds, the main source of information for generating scenarios for pre-loss policy analysis is an analysis of common policy exclusions.

III. Examining policy conditions can help the insurance professional clarify whether the post-loss duties of the insured and the insurer affect coverage.

IV. After using the DICE method to determine whether a claim is covered by a policy, the next step is for the insurer to determine the amount payable.

(A) I and II only

(B) II only

(C) III only

(D) III and IV only

Answer

II. For most insureds, the primary source of information for generating scenarios for pre-loss policy analysis is past loss experience.

The correct answer is (B) II only.

17.3. Policy Analysis

Which of the following statements is not true with regard to the Policy Analysis?

A family's home is destroyed by a fire. A claims adjuster for the home's insurer tries to determine whether the loss was covered by the family's homeowners policy. The claims adjuster would follow the steps specified in the DICE decision tree to determine whether the family's homeowners policy covered the loss.

(A) First, he or she would check the declarations to see whether anything there would preclude coverage. If not, he or she would go to the next step.

(B) Second, he or she would see whether anything in the insuring agreement would preclude coverage. If not, he or she would go to the next step.

(C) Third, he or she would check the conditions to see whether anything precluded coverage and, if not, go to the next step.

(D) Fourth, he or she would check the exclusions and all other policy provisions not already analyzed, including the endorsements and miscellaneous provisions, to make sure that nothing would preclude coverage. If not, he or she would determine whether the post-lost duties of the insured affect coverage.

Answer

(D) If not, he or she would determine the amount payable under the policy.

The correct answer is (D).

SECTION 7. Insurance Policy Analysis

SECTION 8. COMMON POLICY CONCEPTS

Topic 18: Insurable Interests and Insurance to Value

Topic 19: Property and Liability Valuation

Topic 20: Deductibles and Other Sources of Recovery

Topic 18: Insurable Interests and Insurance to Value

CPCU 500 Review Notes / Assignment 8. Common Policy Concepts / EO 1, 2

18.a. When and Why Insurable Interest Is Required

Insurable interest is an interest in the subject of an insurance policy that would cause the interested party to suffer financial loss if an insured event occurred. The requirement for an insurable interest is an issue of law and exists even in the lack of policy provisions specifically addressing insurable interest.

The requirement for insurable interest is different in property-casualty insurance compared to life insurance. ① In life insurance, the beneficiary must have an insurable interest in the life of the insured when the policy is purchased, but not necessarily at the time of the insured's death. ② Insurable interest in property-casualty insurance must be existing at the time of the loss.

Insurance policies have an insurable interest requirement for these three reasons: ① It supports the principle of indemnity. ② It prevents the use of insurance as a wagering mechanism. ③ It reduces the moral hazard incentive that insurance may create for the insured.

18.b. Legal Bases for Insurable Interest

1. Ownership interest in property	Ownership rights to both tangible and intangible property have economic value and are guaranteed and protected by law.
2. Contractual obligations	① Contractual rights regarding people: A contract may provide one party the right to bring a claim against a second party without entitling the first party to any specific property that belongs to the second party. (for example, credit card debts) ② Contractual rights regarding property: Some contracts allow one party to make a claim against specific property held by a second party (for example, a mortgage).
3. Exposure to legal liability	Sometimes one party can have legal responsibility for property owned by others. (For example, a hotelier has an insurable interest in guests' property.) The extent of that insurable interest is the property's full value, including the owner's use value.
4. Factual expectancy	The party need only demonstrate potential financial harm resulting from the event to be insured.
5. Representation of another party	Insurable interest can be based on one party acting as a representative of another party (for example, an agent or trustee). In this case, the representative can obtain insurance on property for the benefit of the property's owner.

18.c. Multiple Parties With Insurable Interests

Joint tenancy	Each owner, termed as a "tenant," owns the whole property and has a right of survivorship: an automatic right of one tenant to the share of the other tenant when that other tenant dies.
	Because anyone joint tenant could turn into the property's sole owner, each tenant has an insurable interest in the property's whole value.
Tenancy by the entirety	This is joint tenancy between a husband and wife. As with a joint tenancy, if spouses jointly own a property, each of them owns the entire property.
Tenancy in common	This is a concurrent ownership of property, in equal or unequal shares, by 2 or more owners.
	Tenants in common do not have survivorship rights. Each party's insurable interest is restricted to that owner's share of the property and any insurance payouts may possibly be made to the first named insured.
Tenancy in partnership	This is concurrent ownership by a partnership and its individual partners regarding personal property used by the partnership.
	The partnership and all partners have rights of survivorship. Both the partnership entity and the individual partners have an insurable interest in property utilized by the partnership. Each partner, and the partnership, would have an interest worth the entire insurable amount.

18.d. Insurance to Value

An essential goal of insurers selling property insurance is to motivate each insured to purchase a limit of insurance that approximates the total value of the covered property, commonly called "insurance to value."

When property is insured to value, the insurer benefits because ① the premium is adequate to cover potential losses and ② it simplifies the underwriting process by reducing the need to determine exact values during underwriting.

The insured benefits from insurance to value because sufficient funds are available in the event of a total loss and the uncertainty associated with large retained losses is reduced.

18.e. How Insurers Encourage Insurance to Value

As an incentive for insuring to value, many policies include insurance-to-value provisions that reduce the amount payable for both partial and total losses if the insured has not purchased adequate limits of coverage. These provisions, which include coinsurance clauses and similar provisions, serve a dual purpose: ① rewarding those who have insured to value and ② penalizing those who have not.

18.f. Coinsurance Clause

Many commercial property insurance policies contain coinsurance clauses, which will make the insured responsible for retaining portion of any loss if the property is under insured below some specified proportion of the property's insurable value. The insurable value is the actual cash value (ACV), the replacement cost value, or whatever other valuation basis applies, in line with the policy's valuation clause.

The most typical coinsurance percentages for buildings and business personal property are 80, 90, and 100 percent. Coinsurance is calculated as "did over should times loss."

18.g. Insurance-to-Value Provisions in HO and BOP policies

Insurance-to-value provisions in homeowners (HO) and businessowners (BOP) policies also encourage insureds to purchase adequate limits.

Under the HO and BOP insurance-to-value provisions, the amount payable by the insurer will be one of these amounts: ① The replacement cost value of the property-effectively, a reward for those insured to at least 80 percent of the replacement cost value of the property ② The actual cash value of the property-effectively, a penalty for those not insured to at least 80 percent of replacement cost value of the property ③ An amount between the replacement cost value and the ACV of the property, determined by the same "did over should times loss" formula used in the coinsurance penalty, with which the loss amount is on a replacement cost basis.

18.h. Insurance-to-Value Problems

Maintaining insurance to value avoids coinsurance penalties and other insurance-to-value provision penalties that might reduce the amount payable in the event of a loss.

Reasons that insureds have difficulty maintaining appropriate property limits include these: ① The amount of insurance necessary to meet coinsurance requirements is based on the insured property's value at the time of the loss, but the policy limit is selected when the policy is purchased. ② When selecting insurance limits, an insurance buyer typically estimates property values based on an informed guess. ③ The insurable value at the time of the loss often cannot be precisely measured until the property is actually rebuilt or replaced. ④ Values change over time.

18.i. Minimizing Insurance-to-Value Problems

Insurance professionals can help property insurance buyers minimize problems associated with valuation by recommending that they take these steps: ① Hire a qualified appraiser to establish the property's current replacement cost value and set policy limits accordingly. ② Review and revise policy limits periodically to ensure that they are adequate to cover potential losses. ③ Consider appropriate coverage options-for example, agreed value optional coverage, inflation guard protection, and the peak season endorsement.

Agreed value optional coverage: Optional coverage that suspends the Coinsurance condition in the event the insured carries the amount of insurance agreed to by the insurer and insured.

Inflation guard protection: A technique for protecting against inflation by increasing the applicable limit for covered property by a specified percentage over the policy period.

Peak season endorsement: Endorsement that covers the fluctuating values of business personal property through providing differing amounts of insurance for certain time periods during the policy period.

18.1. Insurable Interests

Which of the following statements is true with regard to the Insurable Interests?

I. Stephanie, Riley, and Jessica have concurrent ownership in a bistro, each owning one third. Their combined interests equal the value of the bistro. If one of them should die, her share would pass to her heirs. This type of ownership is referred to as tenancy in common.

II. Hugh, Sara, Ron and Laura concurrently own and operate a tavern. Each of them has rights of survivorship and an insurable interest worth the full value of the business. This type of ownership is referred to as joint tenancy.

III. Janet, who owns a dry cleaning establishment, maintains insurance on customers' clothing and other property. She does so because she is serving as a bailee of customers' property while it is in her possession. In cases where a customer's property becomes damaged while in her care, Janet will pay any insurance proceeds to the customer. Factual expectancy is the legal basis for insurable interest demonstrated by this example.

(A) I only

(B) I and II only

(C) III only

(D) All of the above

Answer

II. This type of ownership is referred to as tenancy in partnership, because they own and operate a tavern business.

III. Exposure to legal liability or Representation of another party can be the legal basis for insurable interest demonstrated by this example.

The correct answer is (A) I only.

18.2. Insurable Interests

Which of the following statements is not true with regard to the Insurable Interests?

Versoxy Hospital has hired Longzimong Construction Management as an agent to solicit bids from construction firms for constructing a parking garage within the hospital's premises and to handle all communications with the construction firm selected. Longzimong has awarded the bid for construction to Zest Construction Company. Versoxy has signed a construction loan contract and supreme mortgage commitment with Eastern Financial. Zest has started construction of the garage. The new parking garage is now being constructed in the location of the former employee parking lot. During the construction, employees of Versoxy Hospital must park in an overflow parking lot one block from the hospital.

(A) Longzimong has an agent interest in the parking garage as a representative of Versoxy.

(B) Zest has a contractual obligation to Versoxy and Longzimong that creates an interest in the parking garage.

(C) Eastern has a contractual obligation with Versoxy that creates an interest (as secured creditor) in the parking garage.

(D) Versoxy Hospital employees has a factual expectancy that creates an interest in the parking garage.

Answer

(D) Versoxy Hospital employees has no insurable interest in the parking garage.

The correct answer is (D).

18.3. Insurance to Value

Which of the following statements is not true with regard to the Insurance to Value?

I. With insurance-to-value provisions under homeowners (HO) and businessowners (BOP) policies, the amount payable by the insurer will never be less than the actual cash value (ACV) of the damaged property, subject to policy limits.

II. Murphy has a commercial property policy covering his retail store. The policy has an 80% coinsurance clause, and the insurable value of the store is its replacement cost. When the policy was written, the value of the store was $160,000. Assuming the current replacement cost of the store is $150,000, and that it is insured for $120,000, if the store suffers a $30,000 covered loss, Murphy will recover $30,000 under his insurance policy.

III. Brandon has a commercial property policy covering his retail store. The policy has an 80% coinsurance clause, and the insurable value of the store is its replacement cost. When the policy was written, the value of the store was $300,000. Assuming the current replacement cost of the store is $400,000, and that it is insured for $300,000, if the store suffers a $80,000 covered loss, Brandon will recover $80,000 under his insurance policy.

(A) I only

(B) II and III only

(C) III only

(D) All of the above

Answer

III. Coinsurance is calculated as "did over should times loss." In this example "did" is $300,000, "should" is $320,000 (= $400,000 x 0.8) as the insurable value at the time of the loss. Therefore, if the store suffers a $80,000 covered loss, Brandon will recover $75,000 = ($300,000 / $320,000) x $80,000, under his insurance policy

The correct answer is (C) III only.

Topic 19: Property and Liability Valuation

CPCU 500 Review Notes / Assignment 8. Common Policy Concepts / EO 3, 4

19.a. Property Valuation Methods

Actual cash value (ACV)	① Replacement cost minus depreciation: depreciation is based on economic depreciation, not accounting depreciation. ② Market value: the price at which a particular piece of property could be sold on the open market by an unrelated buyer and seller. ③ Broad evidence rule: a court ruling explicitly requiring that all relevant factors be considered in determining actual cash value.
Replacement cost	The cost to repair or replace property using new materials of like kind and quality with no deduction for depreciation.
Agreed value method	A method of valuing property in which the insurer and the insured agree, at the time the policy is written, on the maximum amount that will be paid in the event of a total loss.
Functional valuation method	A valuation method in which the insurer is required to pay no more than the cost to repair or replace the damaged or destroyed property with property that is its functional equivalent.

19.b. Market Value

Market valuation might be useful when property of like kind and quality is unavailable for purchase, such as with antiques, pieces of art, and other collectibles. These kinds of property may be irreplaceable, making replacement cost calculations impossible. Market valuation can be the most accurate way to determine the value of some older or historic buildings constructed with obsolete construction methods and materials.

When handling real property, the land's value must be removed in establishing insurable values because most insurance policies cover buildings and structures but not land.

19.c. Broad Evidence Rule

When the broad evidence rule is used to determine a building's ACV, the following factors are considered: ① Obsolescence ② Building's present use and profitability ③ Alternate building uses ④ Present neighborhood characteristics ⑤ Long-term community plans for the area where the building is located, including urban renewal prospects and new roadway plans ⑥ Inflationary or deflationary trends

19.d. Replacement Cost

Theoretically, replacement cost coverage violates the principle of indemnity. An insured who sustains a loss to old, used property and receives insurance payment for brand new property has profited from the loss.

To reduce the moral hazard, most replacement cost policies payout only after the insured has actually replaced the damaged or destroyed property or, in some instances, only when the loss is a relatively low value. In many policies with replacement cost provisions, the insured has the option of settling the claim based on ACV and then has 180 days to refile the claim on the replacement cost basis. This provides the insured the opportunity to obtain funds from the insurer at the time of loss, use those funds to help pay for the rebuilding, and then collect the full replacement cost value on completion.

19.e. Agreed value method

Some property insurance policies are valued policies, which is not contracts of indemnity. These policies usually cover commercial watercraft, antiques, paintings, and other objects whose value can be challenging to determine.

If a total loss occurs, the insurer will pay the agreed value specified in the policy. Partial losses are paid based upon actual cash value, repair cost, replacement cost, or whatever other valuation method the policy specifies.

The agreed value method does not indicate what the agreed value has to be relative to the true value of the property. The only stipulation is that both parties have to agree to the value in the policy.

19.f. Functional Valuation Method

The functional valuation method is sometimes used when replacing buildings or personal property with property of like kind and quality is not practical as well as when the ACV method does not match insurance needs.

The functional valuation method is typically used with electronics and computers, because new computers may be more functional but less expensive than the models that have to be replaced.

19.g. Valuation of Liability Claims

Unlike property insurance policies, liability insurance policies (or the liability coverage provisions within a multiline policy) usually do not specify how the amount of a covered claim is determined. Under most circumstances, the maximum amount the insurer pays is the lesser of two amounts: ① The compensable amount of the claim ② The applicable policy limits

The compensable amount of the claim is decided by negotiations between the liability insurer and the claimant if the claim can be settled outside of court. If a settlement cannot be attained by the parties involved, the liability claim will go to trial, and the extent of the insured's liability to the claimant is then based on legal principles.

19.h. Compensable Amount of the Claim

The critical issue affecting the valuation of a liability claim is the amount of monetary compensation that will reasonably indemnify the party who incurred the loss. The claimant generally has the burden of proof regarding bodily injury and damage to property. The claimant must establish what losses were proximately caused by the insured.

When property is damaged, the owner may recover these: ① The reasonable cost to repair the property or, if it cannot be repaired, the cost to replace it (its reasonable market value before damage or destruction) ② The damages to compensate for the loss of use of the property for a reasonable period ③ Under certain circumstances, lost profits from the inability to use the damaged or destroyed property.

To evaluate bodily injury claims, an insurance professional will consider the following elements: ① Reasonable and necessary medical expenses incurred and those expected to be incurred in the future ② Type of bodily injury ③ Wage loss or loss of earning capacity because of the bodily injury ④ Other out-of-pocket expenses, such as household assistance ⑤ Current and future pain and suffering resulting from the bodily injury ⑥ Extent and permanency of disability and impairment ⑦ Disfigurement resulting from the bodily injury ⑧ Preexisting conditions that could have contributed to the bodily injury

19.i. Policy Limits

When a liability policy contains multiple limits, the maximum amount payable for a covered claim depends on a complete analysis of the interactions among the various limits.

In addition to covering the claimant's damages, insurers also agree to pay defense costs and various supplementary payments, such as these: ① The cost of surety bonds required in connection with claims ② Court costs taxed against the insured ③ Interest on judgments.

In lots of common policies, defense costs and supplementary payments do not decrease the policy limits. However, after the insurer has paid out the applicable limit(s) for a claim, the insurer's duty to defend and pay supplementary payments ends. In specialty liability policies, the insurer's payments for defense costs and supplementary payments are normally applied to reduce the policy limits.

19.1. Property Valuation Methods

Which of the following statements is true with regard to the Property Valuation Methods?

I.   Actual cash value is the replacement cost minus accounting depreciation.

II. With agreed value policies, whenever loss occurs, the insurer will pay the agreed value specified in the policy.

III. The agreed value method stipulates what the agreed value has to be relative to the true value of the property.

IV. Cindy Jager, owns a 200 year-old historical building that she uses as an art studio. Rebuilding the structure in the event of loss could become difficult due to the antique fixtures and materials used in the original design of the building. Functional valuation is an insurer most likely to use in the property policy covering this property.

(A) I and II only

(B) II only

(C) III and IV only

(D) IV only

Answer

I. In ACV methods, depreciation is based on economic depreciation, not accounting depreciation.

II. If a total loss occurs, the insurer will pay the agreed value specified in the policy. Partial losses are paid based on actual cash value, repair cost, replacement cost, or whatever other valuation method the policy specifies.

III. The agreed value method does not stipulate what the agreed value has to be relative to the true value of the property. The only stipulation is that both parties have to agree to the value in the policy.

The correct answer is (D) IV only.

19.2. Liability Claims Valuation

Which of the following statements is not true with regard to the Liability Claims Valuation?

I.   Usually, in a liability claim, the burden of proof in relation to what bodily injury or property damage losses were proximately caused by the insured belongs to the claimant.

II. In liability claims, both the insured and the insurer have an incentive to reach an out-of-court settlement due to the uncertainty, time, and expense involved in a formal trial.

III. A claimant in a bodily injury or damage to property liability claim has a duty to mitigate loss after an accident.

IV. A liability claimant normally may not recover damages to make up for loss of use of damaged property.

V.   In lots of common policies, defense costs and supplementary payments reduce the policy limits.

  (A) I only

  (B) II and III only

  (C) IV only

  (D) IV and V only

Answer

IV. When property is damaged by liability, the owner may recover these: ① The reasonable cost to repair the property or, if it cannot be repaired, the cost to replace it (its reasonable market value before damage or destruction) ② The damages to compensate for the loss of use of the property for a reasonable period ③ Under certain circumstances, lost profits from the inability to use the damaged or destroyed property.

The correct answer is (C) IV only.

19.3. Liability Claims Valuation

Which of the following statements is not true with regard to the Liability Claims Valuation?

I. An insured with a CGL policy incurs a covered claim for $500,000 in damages. The policy has a $1 million each occurrence limit. Prior claims paid during the same policy period reduced the applicable aggregate limit to $100,000. Because prior claims paid during the same policy period reduced the applicable aggregate limit to $100,000, the insurer's payment will not exceed $100,000.

II. An insured has a directors and officers liability policy with a $1 million policy limit. The insured is held liable for a $975,000 judgment and defense costs totaling $150,000. If the defense costs and supplementary payment reduce the policy limits, the insurer would pay both the $150,000 in defense costs and the $975,000 judgment in full.

(A) I only

(B) II only

(C) All of the above

(D) None of the above

Answer

II. If an insured with a $1 million policy limit were held liable for a $975,000 judgment and defense costs totaling $150,000, the insurer would pay only $850,000 of the judgment after having paid the defense costs. If the insured had a liability policy that covered defense costs in addition to the limits, the insurer would pay both the $150,000 in defense costs and the $975,000 judgment in fulL

The correct answer is (B) II only.

Topic 20: Deductibles and Other Sources of Recovery

CPCU 500 Review Notes / Assignment 8. Common Policy Concepts / EO 5, 6, 7

20.a. Property Deductibles

Deductibles reduce the premiums insurers must charge and ultimately benefit the insured in the following ways: ① Reduce insurers' overall loss costs and loss adjustment expenses ② Provide insureds with risk control incentives ③ Reduce the morale and moral hazard incentive.

A deductible should be large enough to have a obvious financial impact on the insured. Deductibles that are too small do not offer enough financial incentive, and deductibles that are too large defeat the intention of transferring the loss exposure to the insurer.

Premium credits tend to encourage the use of medium-sized deductibles that eliminate dollar trading for small losses however that provide a reliable source of recovery for large losses. Dollar trading is an insurance premium and loss exchange in which the insured pays the insurer premiums for low value losses, and the insurer pays the same dollars back to the insured, after subtracting expenses.

20.b. Liability Deductibles

Deductibles in liability policies are not as effective as they are in property insurance policies. ① Liability insurers want to control liability claims from the outset; therefore, they want to be involved in even small liability claims that may be less than the deductible amount. ② For most liability policies, deductibles would not noticeably reduce premiums because relatively few liability claims involve small amounts that an insurer would be able to avoid with a deductible. ③ The insurer generally has to pay the third-party claimant the full settlement amount and then try to collect the deductible from the insured, who may be unwilling or unable to make the payment.

Deductibles are common with some specialty liability policies, such as those covering professional liability or directors and officers liability, to encourage risk control. Deductibles are also common in bailee legal liability coverages, such as those for warehouses and auto service businesses.

20.c. Self-Insured Retentions (SIR)

Self-insured retention is a dollar amount specified in an insurance policy that the insured must pay before the insurer will make any payment for a claim.

The differences between a deductible and a self-insured retention (SIR) are as follows: ① With a liability insurance deductible, the insurer defends on a first-dollar basis, pays all covered losses, and then bills the insured for the amount of losses up to the deductible. ② With an SIR, the insurer pays only losses that exceed the SIR amount. The insurer does not defend claims below the SIR amount. Consequently, the organization is responsible for adjusting and paying its own losses up to the SIR amount.

20.d. Other Sources of Recovery

These additional sources of compensation may violate the principle of indemnity in that the insured could be indemnified more than once for the amount of loss.

Noninsurance agreements	Individuals and organizations frequently have a contractually enforceable method to obtain recovery that does not involve insurance. Agreements including warranties or bailment agreements can provide compensation in addition to insurance.
Negligent third parties	A party who is injured or whose property is damaged by a negligent third party generally has a right to recover damages from the third party. Recovery from a third party could overlap with any first-party property insurance.
Other insurance in the same policy	Some property and liability policies may provide 2 or more coverages under the same policy. As an example, scheduled personal property attached to a homeowners policy provides coverage for property that is also covered under the unscheduled personal property coverage.
Other insurance in a similar policy	Coverage may overlap because the same party is protected by two or more policies, usually issued by different insurers. For example, multiple insurers issue policies to cover a single building.
Other insurance in a dissimilar policy	A loss is sometimes covered by more than one type of insurance. For example, a restaurant's valet parking activity might be covered under the restaurant's general liability policy or its commercial auto policy.

20.1. Deductibles

Which of the following statements is not true with regard to the Deductibles?

I.   Deductibles in property insurance policies are most effective in reducing insurers' expenses when they are used with coverages in which small, partial losses are common.

II. Property insurance deductibles reduce premium costs by encouraging insureds to prevent or reduce losses.

III. Self-insured retention is a dollar amount specified in an insurance policy that the insured must pay before the insurer will make any payment for a claim.

IV. The insurer loses its right to provide a defense under liability insurance policies that include a deductible.

V.   Before making payments to third-party claimants, liability insurers must first subtract the deductible amount from the agreed-upon settlement.

(A) I only

(B) II and III only

(C) IV and V only

(D) V only

Answer

IV. Under liability policies that include a deductible, the insurer usually pays all defense costs on a first-dollar basis.

V. The insurer must pay third-party claimants in full and then recover the amount of the deductible from the insured.

The correct answer is (C) IV and V only.

20.2. Other Sources of Recovery

Which of the following statements is not true with regard to the Other Sources of Recovery?

I.   Subrogation provisions in policy wordings prevent insureds from collecting from both negligent third parties and their own insurer.

II. If a negligent third party causes injury and the injured party accepts settlement from his or her own insurer, the negligent party's responsibility to pay damages is eliminated.

III. An insured cannot simultaneously hold two policies of the same type with two different insurers.

IV. If an insured's loss is covered under two similar policies, the policy that was issued first must pay the loss.

V.   While on her way to a business appointment, Elenore is involved in an automobile accident. She suffers minor injuries as a result, and is not sure which insurance policy should cover her expenses. She may be able to recover from her personal auto insurer, or from her employer's workers compensation insurer. This is an example of other insurance in dissimilar policies.

(A) I and III only

(B) II and IV only

(C) I and V only

(D) II and IV only

Answer

II. If the injured party accepts settlement from his or her own insurer, the negligent party's responsibility to pay damages is not eliminated.

IV. In situations involving a loss covered by two similar policies with different insurers, the insurers usually share the loss.

The correct answer is (B) II and IV only.

CPCU 500 Exam Guide

CPCU Program Description

Note: The following information refers to the CPCU Experience Booklet from The Institute.

CPCU Course Descriptions

The current program stands at eight examinations—four foundation courses, one elective course and three concentration courses. The core courses continue to reflect the broad-based curriculum of the early program—risk management and insurance principles, operations, regulation, statutory accounting, law, and finance. The elective course increases the relevancy to the individual allowing study in a functional area of their choosing and provides opportunity to earn cross-credit from other Institutes' programs. The concentration courses allow students to deepen their understanding of either commercial lines or personal lines insurance. The core principles of education, ethics, and experience remain strongly intact.

Foundation Courses

CPCU 500—Foundations of Risk Management and Insurance

CPCU 520—Insurance Operations

CPCU 530—Business Law for Insurance Professionals

CPCU 540 — Finance and Accounting for Insurance Professionals

Commercial Concentration Courses

CPCU 551—Commercial Property Risk Management and Insurance

CPCU 552—Commercial Liability Risk Management and Insurance

CPCU 553— Survey of Personal Insurance and Financial Planning

Personal Concentration Courses

CPCU 555— Personal Risk Management and Property-Casualty Insurance

CPCU 556—Financial Planning

CPCU 557—Survey of Commercial Insurance

Elective Courses

AAI 83—Agency Operations and Sales Management

AIC 34—Workers Compensation and Managing Bodily Injury Claims

AIC 31—Property Claim Practices*

AIC 32—Liability Claim Practices*

ARe 144—Reinsurance Principles and Practices

ARM 56—Risk Financing

AU 67—Strategic Underwriting Techniques*

CPCU 560—Financial Services Institutions

ERM 57—Enterprise-Wide Risk Management: Developing and Implementing

CPCU Ethics Requirement

The Institutes believe that the study of ethics is essential to the professional practice of risk management and insurance. By separating the ethics component, students will be able to more effectively study ethics and achieve a greater understanding of the science and art behind ethical decision-making in the context of the insurance business.

The CPCU ethics requirement is satisfied by completing the online module, Ethics and the CPCU Code of Professional Conduct (Ethics 312), or by having credit for CPCU 510, prior to March 15, 2011.

CPCU Experience Requirement

The CPCU experience requirement is two years. The two-year experience requirement applies to all CPCU students and candidates who qualify for the class of 2010 and beyond, regardless of when the individual started in the program.

CPCU Exam Information and Registration

Note: The following information refers to the CPCU Registration Booklet from The Institute.

Exam Dates

Testing Windows for Computer Administered Institutes Exams

- January 15-March 15
- April 15-June 15
- July 15-September 15
- October 15-December 15

Exam Format

Exams are administered on computer. Computer administered exams are preceded by an optional 30-minute tutorial and are followed by a brief survey.

Category	Number and Type of Questions	Time Limit
ARe, ARM	60-85 multiple-choice questions	2 hours
CPCU 500	60 multiple-choice questions	1.5 hours
CPCU 520, 530, 540, 551, 552, 553, 555, 556, and 557	85 multiple-choice questions	2 hours
CPCU 560	25-35 short essay questions	3 hours

All the above exams have passing grade of 70 percent.

Testing Centers

Computer exams are administered at Prometric Testing Centers and at Institutes-approved on-site testing centers, usually an employer facility. Prometric centers are located in more than 420 cities worldwide. Log on to www.prometric.com/TheInstitutes to find a center. Examinees must arrive at Prometric Testing Centers at least 30 minutes before a scheduled appointment for check-in.

Registering for an Exam

Online www.TheInstitutes.org

Phone (800) 644-2101 (Monday–Friday, 8 am to 6 pm EST)

Fax (610) 640-9576

Mail 720 Providence Rd., Suite 100,

Malvern, PA 19355-3433

Exam Fee

CPCU 520, Oct 15 - Ded 15, 2015 for example

	Institutes Approved On-Site Testing Centers Register through Dec 15, 2015	Prometric Test Center Early Registration Register on or before Oct 15, 2015	Prometric Test Center Standard Registration Register after Oct 15, 2015
Exam Fee:	$240	$260	$330
Registrations accepted through:	Dec 15, 2015	Oct 15, 2015	Dec 12, 2015
Cancellation deadline	Dec 15, 2015	You must cancel 3 or more business days prior to your scheduled Prometric appointment	You must cancel 3 or more business days prior to your scheduled Prometric appointment
Cancellation Forfeiture	$135	$175	$175
Cost to Transfer:	$85	$110	$110

Payment

The Institutes accept American Express, Diners Club, Discover, MasterCard, and VISA. Mailed registrations also may be paid by check or money order. Fees are nonrefundable and nontransferable and must be paid in U.S. currency.

Scheduling a Computer-Administered Exam Appointment

Schedule your appointment when you know you will be ready to sit for the exam. Prometric will charge a $50 fee to students who reschedule their appointments within 3 to 12 business days of a test date. Also, scheduling an appointment far in advance and then canceling could deprive another examinee of a desired testing date and time. Be considerate of others. Still, we also recommend scheduling the exam appointment early in the testing window in case the exam must be rescheduled or retaken.

To locate a Prometric Testing Center and schedule an appointment, log on to www.prometric.com/TheInstitutes or call (877) 311-2525. Prometric's international phone numbers are listed below.

Region	Contact Center	Region	Contact Center
North America–U.S. & Canada	1-877-311-2525	Korea	82-2-1566-0990
Latin America & Caribbean	1-443-751-4995	China	86-10-6279-9911
Europe Middle East & North Africa	31-320-239-540 31-320-239-530	Hong Kong Southeast Asia	60-3-7628-3333 60-3-7628-3333
Africa	31-320-239-593	India	91-124-414-7700
Japan	81-3-5541-4800	Australia & New Zealand	61-2-9640-5899

Taking an Exam

Note: The following information refers to the CPCU Registration Booklet from The Institute.

Exam Policies: Identification

You must present valid, unexpired identification that contains BOTH a photograph and a signature. The name on your ID must exactly match your name as it appears on the examination confirmation notice. If, for example, your identification and confirmation notice do not match because you recently married, bring the original copy of your marriage license. Contact The Institutes at least one week before your appointment if you have any questions about proper ID. If you are denied admission to a testing center because of a question about your ID, immediately call The Institutes at (800) 644-2101 or (610) 644-2100. Do not leave the testing center without calling The Institutes.

Examinee Conduct

CPCUs and CPCU candidates are subject to the CPCU Code of Professional Conduct. The CPCU code is available at www.TheInstitutes.org/doc/Canons.pdf.

CPCUs, along with all other persons taking Institutes exams, are subject to The Institutes' Code of Academic and Professional Integrity. The Institutes' Code is available at www.TheInstitutes.org/CAPI.

Furthermore, you will not be permitted to sit for an exam if you do not agree to abide by the Rules of Conduct statement at the beginning of exam administration and will forfeit the registration fee.

Prohibited Items

Food and drink, jackets and hats, study materials, notes, dictionaries, and any form of electronic device, with the exception of an acceptable calculator (see below), are expressly prohibited. Medical or dietary needs that are taken to a Prometric Testing Center must be submitted to the Institutes for prior approval by Prometric, at least one month before the anticipated testing date. Send a full explanation of your needs to assessments@TheInstitutes.org. A PDA or cell phone cannot be used in place of an acceptable calculator. Lockers are available at Prometric Testing Centers for storing personal items. Do not bring anything to a Prometric Testing Center that you hesitate to place in a locker. Prometric Testing Centers reserve the right to ask examinees to turn out their pockets.

Provided Items for Electronic Exams

Scratch paper and a pencil will be provided and will be collected at the end of the exam. Answers written on scratch paper, but not entered into the computer, are not graded. Ear plugs and a basic calculator are available upon request at Prometric Testing Centers.

Use of a Calculator

Based on the content of their study materials, examinees should determine for themselves whether they need a calculator during an examination. Although a financial calculator is not required for an exam, use of any solar- or battery-powered calculator that does not have alphabetic keys for typing words and that does not contain paper tape is permitted during an exam. Business/financial calculators—including those that are programmable—meeting these criteria are permitted.

A PDA or cell phone is not an acceptable calculator. Prometric will provide a basic calculator if requested. Call the Institutes (800) 644-2101 if you encounter a problem concerning use of an acceptable calculator.

Problems During the Exam

Raise your hand if you encounter a problem during the exam. You may not communicate with anyone other than the test administrator.

Breaks

No scheduled breaks are provided. However, examinees may visit the restroom. When doing so, you will be required to sign out and then sign in again. You must return to your exam within five minutes, and the examination clock will continue to run. Communication with anyone other than a test administrator is prohibited.

Prometric's Test Security Procedures

Security at Prometric Testing Centers is very stringent. You could be asked to turn your pockets out to ensure they are empty. Cameras and video recording are in constant use. Test Center administrators circulate within the testing room at least every 30 minutes. Scratch paper is collected at the end of the exam and shredded.

Information About Computer-Administered Exams

Demo Exam For a hands-on demonstration of computer delivered essay or objective exam questions, visit The Institutes' Web site at www.TheInstitutes.org. Click on Exam Preparation/Grade Information under the Examinations tab and download the exam demo software to your computer.

Taking an Institutes exam on a computer does not require special computer skills. For objective exams, you can use a mouse or the keyboard to indicate an answer. To select your answer by using the keyboard, hold down the Alt key and then press the A, B, C, or D key. When taking an essay-style exam, enter your answers using the computer keyboard. Shortcuts commonly associated with Word processing software are not available.

You can Mark for Review any questions that you want to come back to later. You can set the review screen to show several options, such as which questions were answered and marked or just those that remain unanswered. You can practice Mark for Review with the Demo Exam.

Clicking on the Reference tab will allow you to access documents and formulas that will assist in answering exam questions. The tab will not appear in all exams and will display only in Part B of an examination. Not every exam calls for reference material.

Exam Grading

Multiple-Choice Exams: As soon as you complete the exam, you will receive an unofficial pass/nonpass notification, unless grading is delayed.

Essay Exams: Essay exams are returned to The Institutes for grading. As many as three graders may independently review an exam to determine the final score. Grades are available within one month of the test date, unless grading is delayed.

When registering, please provide The Institutes with a current e-mail address to ensure prompt grade notification. A notice sent to your preferred e-mail address will inform you that an official grade report is available on The Institutes' website. Be advised that spam filters and firewalls could result in the inability to deliver the grade notification.

THE END

CPSIA information can be obtained at www.ICGtesting.com
Printed in the USA
BVOW09s0832151215

30328BV00006B/631/P